Macmillan Computer Science Series

Consulting Editor: Professor F.H. Sumner, University of Manchester

A. Abdellatif, J. Le Bihan and M. Limame, *Oracle – A user's guide*
S.T. Allworth and R.N. Zobel, *Introduction to Real-time Software Design, second edition*
Ian O. Angell, *High-resolution Computer Graphics Using C*
Ian O. Angell and Gareth Griffith, *High-resolution Computer Graphics Using FORTRAN 77*
Ian O. Angell and Gareth Griffith, *High-resolution Computer Graphics Using Pascal*
M. Azmoodeh, *Abstract Data Types and Algorithms, second edition*
C. Bamford and P. Curran, *Data Structures, Files and Databases*
Philip Barker, *Author Languages for CAL*
A.N. Barrett and A.L. Mackay, *Spatial Structure and the Microcomputer*
R.E. Berry, B.A.E. Meekings and M.D. Soren, *A Book on C, second edition*
P. Beynon-Davies, *Information Systems Development*
G.M. Birtwistle, *Discrete Event Modelling on Simula*
B.G. Blundell and C.N. Daskalakis, *Using and Administering an Apollo Network*
B.G. Blundell, C.N. Daskalakis, N.A.E. Heyes and T.P. Hopkins, *An Introductory Guide to Silvar Lisco and HILO Simulators*
T.B. Boffey, *Graph Theory in Operations Research*
Richard Bornat, *Understanding and Writing Compilers*
Linda E.M. Brackenbury, *Design of VLSI Systems – A Practical Introduction*
Alan Bradley, *Peripherals for Computer Systems*
G.R. Brookes and A.J. Stewart, *Introduction to occam 2 on the Transputer*
J.K. Buckle, *Software Configuration Management*
W.D. Burnham and A.R. Hall, *Prolog Programming and Applications*
P.C. Capon and P.J. Jinks, *Compiler Engineering Using Pascal*
J.C. Cluley, *Interfacing to Microprocessors*
J.C. Cluley, *Introduction to Low Level Programming for Microprocessors*
Robert Cole, *Computer Communications, second edition*
Derek Coleman, *A Structured Programming Approach to Data*
E. Davalo and P. Naïm, *Neural Networks*
S.M. Deen, *Fundamentals of Data Base Systems*
S.M. Deen, *Principles and Practice of Database Systems*
C. Delannoy, *Turbo Pascal Programming*
Tim Denvir, *Introduction to Discrete Mathematics for Software Engineering*
D. England *et al.*, *A Sun User's Guide*
A.B. Fontaine and F. Barrand, *80286 and 80386 Microprocessors*
J.B. Gosling, *Design of Arithmetic Units for Digital Computers*
M.G. Hartley, M. Healey and P.G. Depledge, *Mini and Microcomputer Systems*
J.A. Hewitt and R.J. Frank, *Software Engineering in Modula-2 – An Object-oriented Approach*
Roger Hutty, *COBOL 85 Programming*
Roger Hutty, *Z80 Assembly Language Programming for Students*
Roland N. Ibbett and Nigel P. Topham, *Architecture of High Performance Computers, Volume I*
Roland N. Ibbett and Nigel P. Topham, *Architecture of High Performance Computers, Volume II*
Patrick Jaulent, *The 68000 – Hardware and Software*
P. Jaulent, L. Baticle and P. Pillot, *68020–30 Microprocessors and their Coprocessors*
M.J. King and J.P. Pardoe, *Program Design Using JSP – A Practical Introduction*
E.V. Krishnamurthy, *Introductory Theory of Computer Science*
V.P. Lane, *Security of Computer Based Information Systems*

(continued overleaf)

A.M. Lister and R.D. Eager, *Fundamentals of Operating Systems, fourth edition*
Elizabeth Lynch, *Understanding SQL*
Tom Manns and Michael Coleman, *Software Quality Assurance*
A. Mével and T. Guéguen, *Smalltalk-80*
R.J. Mitchell, *Microcomputer Systems Using the STE Bus*
R.J. Mitchell, *Modula-2 Applied*
Y. Nishinuma and R. Espesser, *UNIX – First contact*
Pim Oets, *MS-DOS and PC-DOS – A Practical Guide, second edition*
A.J. Pilavakis, *UNIX Workshop*
Christian Queinnec, *LISP*
E.J. Redfern, *Introduction to Pascal for Computational Mathematics*
Gordon Reece, *Microcomputer Modelling by Finite Differences*
W.P. Salman, O. Tisserand and B. Toulout, *FORTH*
L.E. Scales, *Introduction to Non-Linear Optimization*
Peter S. Sell, *Expert Systems – A Practical Introduction*
A.G. Sutcliffe, *Human–Computer Interface Design*
Colin J. Theaker and Graham R. Brookes, *A Practical Course on Operating Systems*
M.R. Tolhurst *et al.*, *Open Systems Interconnection*
J-M. Trio, *8086 – 8088 Architecture and Programming*
A.J. Tyrrell, *COBOL from Pascal*
M.J. Usher, *Information Theory for Information Technologists*
B.S. Walker, *Understanding Microprocessors*
Colin Walls, *Programming Dedicated Microprocessors*
I.R. Wilson and A.M. Addyman, *A Practical Introduction to Pascal – with BS6192, second edition*

Non-series

Roy Anderson, *Management, Information Systems and Computers*
I.O. Angell, *Advanced Graphics with the IBM Personal Computer*
J.E. Bingham and G.W.P. Davies, *Planning for Data Communications*
B.V. Cordingley and D. Chamund, *Advanced BASIC Scientific Subroutines*
N. Frude, *A Guide to SPSS/PC+*
Percy Mett, *Introduction to Computing*
Barry Thomas, *A PostScript Cookbook*

Neural Networks

Eric Davalo and Patrick Naïm

Translated by Λ. Rawsthorne
Department of Computer Science
University of Manchester

MACMILLAN

© The Macmillan Press Ltd 1991
© Editions Eyrolles 1990

Authorised English language edition of *Des Reseaux
de Neurones*, by E. Davalo and P. Naïm, published by
Editions Eyrolles, Paris 1991

First published 1991 by
THE MACMILLAN PRESS LTD
Houndmills, Basingstoke, Hampshire RG21 2XS
and London
Companies and representatives
throughout the world

ISBN 0–333–54996–1

A catalogue record for this book is available
from the British Library.

Printed in Hong Kong

Reprinted 1992

Contents

Contents   ix

Foreword

The brain has a long history in the development of different species. It has evolved in size and in neurological complexity over many millions of years; from fish to amphibians, and from reptiles to the mammals, the story of vertebrates is that of a constant struggle to escape from the seas and conquer dry land. This long march, needing constant adaptation to a sometimes hostile environment, was made possible by the development of the brain, giving more precise sensory inputs, allowing coordination and even planning of future actions. At the same time, paradoxically, the brain has remained a mystery to man himself, and all the great thinkers since the Greeks have advanced their own theories to explain its operation.

Since the 1940s, it seems that a quiet revolution has taken place in this domain, made possible by the joint efforts of biology, cognitive studies and engineering. In the 1940s, one school of thought, following Von Neumann, Wiener, Turing and McCulloch, attempted to lay down the foundations of a science of self-organising systems. Wiener proposed the name 'Cybernetics' for this science. In 1943, McCullough and Pitts proposed a model for a nerve cell, or neuron, using a threshold device they called a 'formal neuron'. Some years later, Rosenblatt had the idea of arranging these devices into a network, conceiving the perceptron. This early system was capable of recognising simple shapes. Widrow designed the 'Adaline' machine, which was used for the recognition of speech. After having raised high hopes, this first direction of research was substantially abandoned following the work of Minsky and Papert, who brought the severe limitations of the perceptron to light. Workers in artificial intelligence then started a new school of thought, following Simon, Chomsky, Minsky and McCarthy, addressing the problem of symbolic manipulation, based on the hypothesis that thought processes could be modelled using a set of symbols and applying a set of logical transformation rules. Using computers as investigative tools, this approach had an enormous success, and started the development of artificial intelligence. This work was very fruitful, giving rise to important new concepts, and allowing expert systems to be applied in a number of different semantic domains, albeit in well-defined problem areas.

Nevertheless, this symbolic approach has a number of limitations. One is the speed of the sequential methods in use; it is difficult to parallelise them, and when the quantity of data increases, the methods may suffer a combinatorial explosion.

A second weakness concerns the representation of knowledge: this is localised, in the sense that one item of knowledge is represented by a precise object, perhaps a byte in memory, or a production rule. These two weaknesses simply do not appear in the neural network, or connectionist approach. In the first case, the fundamental operation of these networks is parallel, and secondly, knowledge representation is distributed: one fact may correspond to activity in a number of neurons. This non-localised means of representing information implies a certain resistance to damage.

A third weakness of the symbolic approach concerns learning. In spite of great efforts by many research teams, it seems difficult to simulate the learning process in a symbolic system. The connectionist approach exhibits learning very clearly. Learning a fact is carried out by reinforcing connections between the neurons which store that fact, and the network organises itself using the examples which are presented to it.

To summarise, the connectionist approach offers the following advantages over the symbolic approach:

o parallel and real-time operation of many different components;

o the distributed representation of knowledge;

o learning by modifying connection weights.

These advantages drove the researchers of the 1980s to re-evaluate the connectionist approach. Neural networks became a useful topic again.

The two approaches are both currently being investigated, and the future will undoubtedly bring attempts to combine them, using connectionism to tackle low-level functions such as pattern recognition, and the symbolic methods to model, combine and supervise different areas of self-organisation, and carrying out syntheses at different levels of abstraction.

At the Ecole Centrale de Paris, the Applied Mathematics group and its associated laboratory have played a part in this story, having introduced an area of study into symbolic manipulation closely linked to the classical themes of applied mathematics. The weaknesses of the symbolic approach were recognised early, and in 1988 it was decided to create a research group into 'bionetworks and parallel computation'. In its initial conception, this group clearly shows the multidisciplinary nature of neural network study. The group has introduced lecturers such as M. Burnod, from the Institut Pasteur, and Mme. Fogelman, from the Ecole des Hautes Etudes en Informatique, for students studying both bioengineering and applied mathematics.

My thanks go to the two authors of this work, M. Davalo and M. Naïm, who have shared in the introduction of these courses, giving associated lectures and supervising practical work, essential to illustrate the concepts. The presentation of their book is lively, clearly showing the problem areas and describing the families of algorithms corresponding to actual solutions.

   I think that anyone desiring to learn about the subject of neural networks will find this book a good introduction, showing how the increasingly abundant literature on the subject can be approached. Returning to the introductory phrases of this foreword, readers will be able to take part themselves in this great saga of the vertebrates, never fully satisfied with their actual position, always ready to escape to further horizons.

F.M. Clément
Professeur at the Ecole Centrale
Head of Applied Mathematics option
and of the M.A.S. Laboratory
(Applied Mathematics and Systems)

Preface

The term 'neural networks' is used to describe a number of different models intended to imitate some of the functions of the human brain, using certain of its basic structures. The historical origins of this study area are very diverse.

In 1943, McCulloch and Pitts studied a collection of model neurons and showed that they were capable of calculating certain logical functions. Hebb, in a psycho-physiological study published in 1949, pointed out the importance of the connection between synapses to the process of learning.

Rosenblatt described the first operational model of neural networks in 1958, putting together the ideas of Hebb, McCulloch and Pitts. His perceptron, inspired by studies of the visual system, could *learn* to calculate logical functions by modifying the connections between its own synapses. This model stimulated a great deal of research at the time, and certainly gave rise to over-optimistic hopes.

When two mathematicians, Minsky and Papert, demonstrated the theoretical limits of the perceptron in 1969, the effect was dramatic: researchers lost interest in neural networks, and turned to the symbolic approach to artificial intelligence, which seemed much more promising at the time.

The recent resurgence of interest in neural networks is largely due to individual contributions such as that of Hopfield, who showed the analogy between neural networks and certain physical systems in a 1982 study, bringing a rich and well understood formalism to bear on these networks. More recently, since 1985, new mathematical models have enabled the original limits of the perceptron to be greatly extended.

Today, the first practical applications of neural networks are beginning to see the light of day, and the discipline is beginning to interest a larger and larger audience of students, researchers, engineers and industrialists.

However, as a result of the multi-disciplinary nature of the subject, it is very difficult to learn about neural networks in a coherent manner. Many thousands of papers have been published on the subject in journals covering biology, psychology, mathematics, physics and electronics, each approaching the problem from its own particular specialist direction.

This book is based upon the authors' own experience of these difficulties; its aim is to convey an intuitive and practical understanding of neural networks and to provide the foundations necessary before undertaking further study. To this end, the first part of this book is devoted to a description of biological foundations. Biology is the source of study of neural networks and it seems probable that it will continue to provide a source of essential ideas. Following this introduction, a general model for neural networks is presented and a number of today's most important models are studied. Lastly, a number of real applications are discussed.

In conclusion, the authors hope that reading this book will enable readers to imagine a possible application for neural networks in their own area of interest, and to experiment further.

1 *Biological Foundations*

The first part of this book begins by presenting a brief history of the study of the brain. Following this is a description of the principal components of the nervous system, with the aim of explaining the models introduced in later portions of the book, without pretending to be exhaustive. Lastly, the brain as a whole is considered, and we try to show how parts of its behaviour may follow from the description of its structure.

1.1 Background

1.1.1 The History of the Study of the Brain

The Heart or the Brain

The dispute which occupied the ancient Greeks over the respective roles of the heart and the brain took about 3,000 years before being resolved. Some philosophers thought the heart the place in which sentiment and intelligence resided. In their time, both Homer and Aristotle, the medieval thinkers and some as late as Descartes felt that the flow of blood from the heart to the brain served the purpose of producing 'animal spirits' which animated the body.

Not until the 18th century was the theory of the role of the brain as the central source of commands to the organism as a whole recognised in Europe. This theory was asserted by La Mettrie and Cabanis in a work called 'The Brain Secretes Thought as the Liver Secretes Bile'; this was after some centuries of obscuration during the medieval period (see [Chan]).

Democritus and then Plato were the first explain this, but the first clinical observations were not carried out until the time of Hippocratus. Herophilus performed the first dissections in the third century BC.

Physiological studies of the brain date back to Galien, who demonstrated with the aid of animal experiments in the second century AD that the brain was definitely the central organ of command in the body.

Research work carried out since the 19th century has given rise to many theories about the operation of the brain.

Methods of Study

Three comments can be made about the different methods of studying the brain.

The method which gave birth to neuro-psychology is based on the study of the relationships between anatomical features and aspects of behaviour. Broca started this work in the 19th century: he began the anatomic-pathological study of language, his work becoming the basis of modern neuro-psychology. Using his own experiences, Broca showed that the motor functions of the brain and its senses are precisely localised in its structure.

This localisation of function gives a good field of study for analytical methods. These methods, however, are criticised by some workers who favour a global approach. They consider them too simplistic to explain systems as complicated as living creatures. Nevertheless, analytical methods have been particularly useful in the study of the visual system, and they remain the basis of all scientific study of the brain today.

Lastly, the most recent area of study is the physical and chemical processes of brain functions. The operation of the brain can be explained in more and more detail, descending closer and closer to the molecular level. The study of the brain has passed from a classification of the parts of the brain responsible for function, to a study of the relationships between behaviour and electrical, then chemical properties.

1.1.2   The Evolution of the Brain

The success of the work of Broca, who demolished the theories of the globalists, gave rise to maps of the brain which are used to describe its evolution in different animal species.

The very first brain on earth appeared in a fish. This brain represents a primitive stage in the evolution of vertebrates. It consisted of three areas, an anterior part, devoted to the sense of smell, a median part whose function was vision, and a posterior part for balance. This brain was incapable of fine nuances of responses or coordinating between its different parts. Each part performed a certain type of behaviour completely determined by responses to certain stimuli.

Species have evolved through a large number of stages from this original fish, before reaching *homo sapiens*. It is interesting to note that, in the evolutionary process, there is a link between the weight of the brain and the total body weight in each newly-evolved species. This is because the brain itself has developed. Firstly, the part of the brain devoted to smell developed in the first small mammals which hunted at night; the development continued with the growth of the cerebral cortex, the location of the higher activities of thought. One conclusion which can be drawn from this evolutionary process is that species with the highest ratio of brain weight to total body weight are best adapted to their environment and these species have progressively come to dominate.

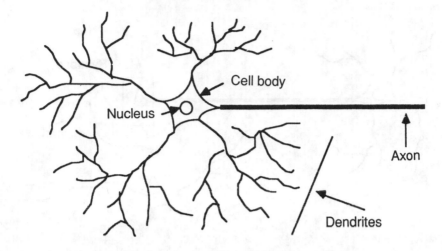

Figure 1.1   Components of a neuron

1.2   The Components of the Brain

1.2.1   The Neuron

Nerve cells, called neurons, are the fundamental elements of the central nervous system. The central nervous system is made up of about 5 billion neurons. Neurons possess a number of points in common with other cells in their general organisation and their biochemical systems, but they also possess a number of distinctive characteristics.

Neurons have five specialist functions: they receive signals coming from neighbouring neurons, they integrate these signals, they give rise to nerve pulses, they conduct these pulses, and they transmit them to other neurons which are capable of receiving them.

Structure of Neurons

A neuron is built up of three parts: the cell body, the dendrites, and the axon, as shown in figure 1.1.

The body of the cell contains the *nucleus* of the neuron and carries out the biochemical transformations necessary to synthesise enzymes and other molecules necessary to the life of the neuron. Its shape in most cases is a pyramid or a sphere. The shape often depends on its position in the brain, so most neurons in the neocortex have a pyramid shape. The cell body is some microns in diameter.

Each neuron has a hair-like structure of *dendrites* around it. These are fine tubular extensions some tenths of a micron across, tens of microns in length. They

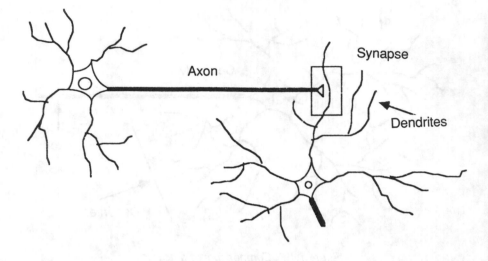

Figure 1.2   The synapse

branch out into a tree-like form around the the cell body. The dendrites are the principal receptors of the neuron and serve to connect its incoming signals.

The *axon* or nerve fibre is the outgoing connection for signals emitted by the neuron. It differs from dendrites in its shape and by the properties of its external membrane. The axon is longer than dendrites, in general, varying from a millimetre to more than a metre in length. It branches at its extremity where it communicates with other neurons, while the branching of dendrites takes place much closer to the cell body.

Neurons are connected one to another in a complex spatial arrangement to form the central nervous system. As shown in figure 1.2, the connection between two neurons takes place at *synapses*, where they are separated by a synaptic gap of the order of one-hundredth of a micron.

Neuron Operation

The specific function performed by a neuron depends on the properties of its external membrane. This fulfils five functions: it serves to propagate electrical impulses along the length of the axon and of its dendrites, it releases transmitter substances at the extremity of the axon, it reacts with these transmitter substances in the dendrites at the cell body, it reacts to the electrical impulses which are transmitted from the dendrites and generates or fails to generate a new electrical pulse, and lastly, it enables the neuron to recognise which other neurons it should be connected to; during the development of the brain it permits the neuron to find those cells.

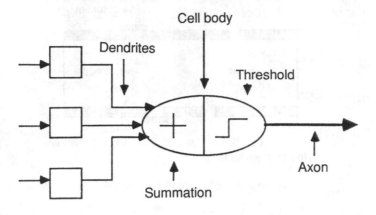

Figure 1.3   The neuron model

The Cell as an Adder with Threshold

A simple description of the operation of a neuron is that it processes the electric currents which arrive on its dendrites and transmits the resulting electric currents to other connected neurons using its axon. The classic biological explanation of this processing is that the cell carries out a summation of the incoming signals on its dendrites. If this summation exceeds a certain threshold, the neuron responds by issuing a new pulse which is propagated along its axon. If the summation is less than the threshold the neuron remains inactive. The pulse which is propagated between different neurons is therefore an electrical phenomenon. This model of a neuron is shown in figure 1.3.

The Origin of Nerve Pulses

The membrane of a neuron serves to maintain a potential difference between the interior of the neuron and the external world. At rest this potential difference is of the order of -70 millivolts. In order to maintain this difference, the neural membrane acts as an ion pump which ejects or attracts certain ions by the use of certain specific channels.

At the cell level, the membrane consists of five types of different channels, making a precise explanation of the biochemical mechanism difficult. Nevertheless, the membrane reacts to the electrical impulses transmitted to it by the dendrites and responds in a manner defined by its different ion pumps. Neurons can fire over a wide range of frequencies, but always fire with the same amplitude. Information transmitted by nerve cells is therefore represented by the number of neuron firing actions produced in a unit of time. In other words, information is frequency encoded on the emitted signals.

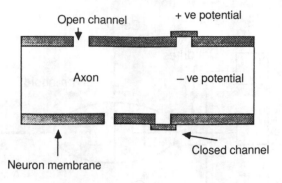

Figure 1.4   Quiescent axon membrane

Nerve Impulse Propagation

The propagation of impulses generated by the body of the neuron cell takes place using the mechanism of ion pumps and channels present in the axonic membrane. The ion pumps maintain a difference in concentration of the sodium and potassium ions between the axon and the external medium. Their role is to expel sodium ions and to capture potassium ions. The channels are distributed along the axonic membrane and serve to permit or deny the passage of sodium or potassium ions.

At rest, when no impulses are being transmitted, the channels are closed and the pumps maintain a negative potential in the axon, as shown in figure 1.4. When a nerve impulse, generated by the cell body, is propagated, the potential difference between the axon and the external medium diminishes. This causes the opening of the sodium channels immediately in advance of the nerve impulse, as shown in figure 1.5. The effect of the entry of sodium ions into the axon is to reverse the previous potential difference, and thus the nerve impulse is propagated further.

The potassium channels open automatically immediately after the opening of the sodium channels. This provokes a re-inversion of the potential in the axon and brings the axon back into its initial electrical state.

In this manner the action potential of the neuron is propagated automatically, and the neuron then recovers its initial state.

Reception of Nerve Impulses by Dendrites

When an action potential arrives at the end of an axon connected to a dendrite by a synapse, it causes the liberation of a chemical transmitter across the membrane at this synapse. This transmitter diffuses to the post-synaptic membrane of the dendrite where, by opening a chemically sensitive channel, it provokes the birth of a potential called the post-synaptic potential. This potential is propagated along the length of the dendrite to the body of the neuron.

Recent research results show that the synapses cannot be considered as simple electrical connections, but must be regarded as semi-autonomous processing

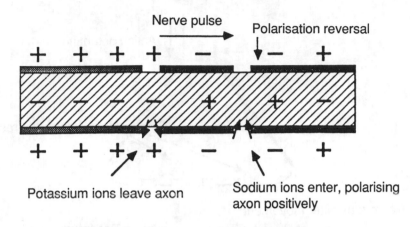

Figure 1.5   Propagating the nerve pulse

sub-units. This research modifies the classic description of dendrites as passive elements connected to the cell body, the only processing unit in the neuron.

It is noteworthy that the shape of the neuron and in particular, the spatial distribution of its dendrites, largely determines the function which the neuron performs.

1.2.2   Synapses

The role of synapses is essential in communication between nerve cells. Signals propagating along cells may be electrical in nature, but there is no direct connection between two nerve cells. They are separated by a space called the *synaptic gap*, which the electrical pulses cannot directly cross. The connection is implemented by the intermediary of a chemical transmitter.

Description

Synapses occur most frequently between axons and dendrites, but they are also found between two dendrites, between an axon and a cell body, or between two axons. In this last case, two different configurations are possible. The end of an axon may modify the synaptic activity between an axon and a dendrite, or else it may be connected directly to the beginning of another axon, giving it a very strong influence on the behaviour of this axon (see [McCl]).

The general function of operation of a synapse, shown in figure 1.6, is as follows. The arrival of an action potential at one of the extremities of the terminal network, called the *terminal button*, releases a chemical substance called a neurotransmitter. This substance diffuses into the synaptic gap and attaches itself to specific receptors (neuroreceptors) sited on the terminations of the target neuron.

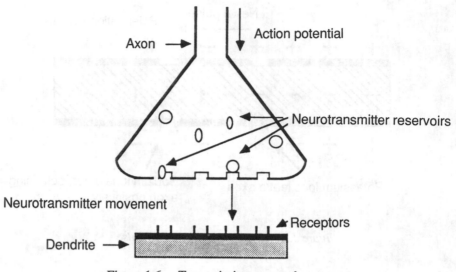

Figure 1.6   Transmission across the synapse

This attachment causes the opening of ion channels which gives rise to a new electrical signal in the receiving dendrite.

Before the arrival of a second pulse, the synaptic gap is cleaned up, either by a recapture of the mediator by the first neuron or by the destruction of the mediator by enzyme action.

It is worth noting the central roles played by the neurotransmitters, permitting the transmission of the signal, and by the neuroreceptors, ensuring the translation of the chemical signal into an electrical signal.

Neurotransmitters

At the synapses, there are a number of types of neurotransmitters. Exciter neurotransmitters act by triggering the destination neuron, producing a new electrical impulse in that target neuron. In particular, acetylcholine is found at the junction between nerve and muscle cells. It acts by causing an inversion of the electric potential in the muscle fibres, triggering their contraction and the movement of the connected body parts.

Inhibitor neurotransmitters act by preventing nerve impulses at the synapses where they are present. In particular GABA acts to prevent abnormal or parasitic movements. The degeneration of certain synaptic sites rich in GABA provokes the illness known as Huntington's Chorea, whose symptoms are almost incessant involuntary movements. Certain neurotransmitters act locally but can also act at a distance; these transmitters are sometimes called neuromodulators.

1.2.3 Support Cells

Apart from the neurons, a number of cells, playing different roles are found within the brain. These roles are support and nutrition, and the set of these cells is covered by the term neurology.

Certain of these support cells have a very specialised role: one example is the Schwann cells. These envelop the axons and form many dense protective layers, called myelin.

The sheath of myelin which surrounds axons is regularly interrupted to form openings through which the sodium and potassium pumps can function. This permits the conduction of action potentials from one opening to another using a form of conduction called saline. This mechanism permits a much faster conduction than continuous conduction and axons surrounded in myelin can be much finer. This also saves energy.

In the frog a nerve fibre sheathed in myelin of 12 micrometres diameter conducts impulses at the speed of 25 metres per second; the same speed as the large, unsheathed axon of a cuttlefish which, with a diameter of 500 micrometres, consumes 5,000 times more energy.

In the human brain, this support structure amounts to about 40 per cent of the brain volume.

1.3 Functional Principles

1.3.1 Central and Hierarchical Control

The concept of an organism's 'internal state' is comparatively recent, dating back to the proposals of Claude Bernard in the last century. This concept expresses the relationship between a living body and an internal state, describing the biological entity of the animal and expressing its autonomy with respect to the external world.

The principle of survival, which motivates every living being, can be explained by the necessity of maintaining this internal state constant in the face of external changes. This process is given the name *homeostasis*. The organism can exhibit responses to changes in the external state which vary the organism's characteristics in order to preserve its internal state (see [Vin]).

The two corollaries of homeostasis are stability and adaptability. Stability arises because the maintenance of a constant internal state allows the organism to resist changes, both external and internal. Adaptability occurs because there can be a cause and effect relationship between external perturbations and the organism's associated regulatory mechanisms.

For homeostasis to operate, the internal state must possess some organisation, and there must be a system of communications, both internal and external. In animals, and in human beings, the central nervous system performs both these roles. The brain performs the function of centralised control, exerting control at different levels to provide both stability and adaptability.

To provide stability, the brain commands and coordinates neuromotor activity under the influence of internal and external information sources. For these purposes, it exhibits a series of responses, each triggered by particular stimuli; it possesses functions to analyse sensory information, permitting it to construct sensible representations of the external world; and it has further functions to analyse internal information to evaluate its own internal state.

To provide adaptability, the brain provides cognitive functions, present in vertebrates and higher invertebrates. It is capable of memory, that is, remembering previous significant events in order to modify or enrich its own sets of actions. It is also capable of imagination, the conceptual representation or simulation of events or actions of the animal itself.

1.3.2   Information from the External World

As previously described, the brain, in its function of central controller of the organism, needs to receive information about the being's environment, the external world, and about the body itself, the internal world. If the latter requirement is not immediately obvious, consider the case of walking or maintaining an upright position. These functions involve the use of parts of the nervous system which inform the brain about the position of different parts of the body and their relationship with each other. For information coming from the external world, the body possesses a set of external receptors.

Sensory Receptors

The brain receives information about the environment through the action of specialised sensory receptors. These receptors may be classified into a number of types, each responding to a different type of stimulus (see [Mes]). There are mechanical receptors responding to pressure and sound, chemical receptors (smell, taste), thermal receptors, electroreceptors and photoreceptors.

Receptors act as transducers which transform a particular type of energy outside the organism (such as light) into internal electrical energy. This takes place by means of a depolarisation of the cell membrane of the receptor; the membrane permeability to certain types of ion varies under the influence of the signal received from the external world. In a similar manner to that described previously for the operation of synapses, in a receptor there is a transformation of signals from the external world into electrical signals which propagate in the nerve cell.

The purpose of these receptors is twofold; first to warn the brain about perceived changes in the environment, and secondly to enrich the contents of the brain by providing input to the memory and by stimulating the organisation of the neural structure and the connections between nerves. This is called plasticity and is a property common to all connections between neurons. Every sensory receptor is placed under the influence of a genetic programme, but its functioning, its adaptation to the needs of the organism, is the result of its interaction with the environment, which modifies the structures and nervous connections (see section 1.3.4).

The Eye

The visual system is perhaps the best understood sensory system. It consists of receptors in the eye, the optic nerve connecting the receptors to the brain, and the visual cortex which plays an important part in the processing of visual information.

The functions of the eye are twofold, seeing and looking, which involves moving the eye to follow something.

The eye is structured so that rays of light arrive, passing initially through the cornea and then the lens. The lens focuses an image of the external world on the retina, which lies at the back of the eye. The image projected on the retina is precise and well focused, activating the light-sensitive part of the eye. This consists of a number of light-sensitive receptors, which are photosensitive nerve cells occurring in the shape of rods or cones.

The rods are found over almost all of the retina. They contain a pigment which is decomposed by light and is only resynthesised slowly (explaining the phenomenon of dazzlement). The cone cells are found essentially only in the centre of the retina. They are sensitive both to shape and to colour.

The image of the world 'seen' by the retina of the eye is thus composed of a series of points, black and white or coloured.

The signals generated by these visual receptor cells are subject to initial processing by nerve cells found at the back of the eye, before being transmitted to the brain. The electrical signals transmitted by the optic nerve pass through a relay centre at the very heart of the brain before ending up in the visual cortex at the rear of the brain.

Hubel and Wiesel have recently shown that the visual cortex is organised as a system of columns of nerve cells extending from the surface to the depths. These columns seem to be the functional units of the cortex, coding the primary data for visual experiences. This subject area is covered in detail in [Bur].

1.3.3 Processing Complex Information

The Visual System of the Frog

To explain how the central nervous system processes complex information about the external world provided by the organism's receptors, we describe the visual system of the frog.

In the frog, the cells which analyse the visual system are found immediately behind the eye. As described below they represent a relatively early stage in the evolution of central nervous systems among animals.

The frog possesses four types of cells whose function is to discriminate only the following different events:

o a moving object penetrates the frog's field of vision;

o a moving object penetrates the field of vision and stops;

o the general level of lighting in the field of vision decreases suddenly;

o a small dark object round in form enters the field of vision of the frog and moves around in an erratic manner.

The first three events put the frog into a state of alert. The first case can be interpreted as the arrival of an intruder. The second case involves the intruder stopping and the danger becoming real. The third case can be interpreted as the arrival of a predator which is overshadowing the frog. All three cases give rise to the 'escape' response.

The last case suggests that an insect is close and it causes an attack by the frog regardless of whether or not there is really prey there.

The responses of the frog, attack or flight, are triggered entirely visually.

The visual signals are processed in the frog just behind the retina by cells which transmit a highly selective form of information to the brain. The brain therefore interprets the external world in terms of events significant for the survival of the frog. The brain of the frog selects a single action as a function of this information.

These responses may be highly complex in terms of the number of primitive muscle movements, but they cannot evolve, showing that the nervous system of the frog functions as an associative filter.

These mechanisms are very limited, although they would be very complicated to program on a traditional computer. For example, a frog is totally incapable of recognising a freshly killed insect suspended just in front of it, showing the limitations of this type of filtering.

The Visual Nervous System of Mammals

The visual system of mammals is better developed and much more complex than that of a frog. The analytical cells are found not just behind the retina, but throughout the visual cortex (see [Mes]).

A study of the effect of stimulating the visual system of a cat using straight lines has enabled the understanding of the more general mechanism used by the brain to decode sensory messages. This research was carried out with the aid of micro-electrodes which permit the measurement of the activity of individual nerve cells (see [Mes]).

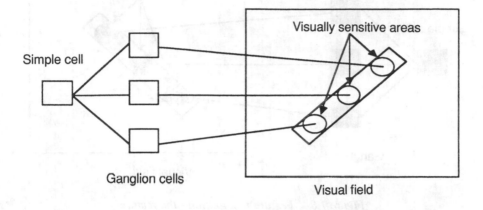

Figure 1.7   Feature recognition - the connections

Three groups of cells can be distinguished by these means: the *ganglion* cells, found just behind the retina, and *simple* and *complex* cells, both found in the visual cortex. Each of these groups plays a specific role in the processing of the cat's visual signals.

The first group of cells divides the received image into a collection of small circular areas each affecting precisely one ganglion cell. The level of illumination of each of these areas is encoded by the level of activity of its associated ganglion cell.

The simple group of cells in the visual cortex performs the same type of di vision of the image, but into larger, more rectangular areas, each containing a number of the circular areas detected by the ganglion cells. The level of activity of the simple cells is influenced by the presence of light or dark lines in the areas which affect them.

Furthermore, the amount of this activity depends on the angle of inclination of the lines, their activity being minimal for the lines at a right angle to those which correspond to their maximum activity. This suggests that the sensitivity of a simple cell to a particular direction depends on the connections between this cell and the ganglion cells.

To explain how these connections operate, figure 1.7 shows one simple cell connected to three ganglion cells which detect certain circular areas in the visual field. The functioning of this system is illustrated by figures 1.8 and 1.9. If all three circular areas are illuminated, the simple cell detects a straight line. If some of the areas are not illuminated, the cell does not detect the line.

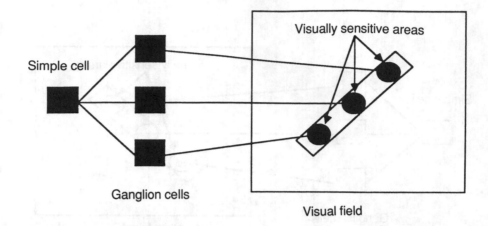

Figure 1.8   Feature recognition - the feature

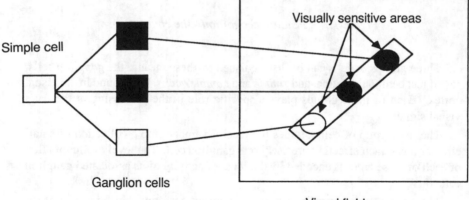

Figure 1.9   Feature recognition - no feature

Complex cells in the visual cortex perform yet higher functions. It is found, for example, that certain of these cells are sensitive to the fact that there is a straight line somewhere in the visual space of the cat, implying that these cells are connected to all of the simple cells detecting individual straight lines at particular places in the image and that they perform the logical OR function over the output of these simple cells.

To summarise these points, the receptor cells on the retina can be seen as responding to a straight line stimulus by exciting certain ganglion cells with receptive areas in the appropriate neighbourhood. These ganglion cells then stimulate the simple cells which are specialised for the recognition of straight lines in particular areas of the visual space, the operation of these cells being a function of their connections to the ganglion cells. Finally, a group of simple cells may be connected to a single complex cell which is activated when any one of these simple cells is triggered.

We conclude that these cells operate in a hierarchical manner and that they extract more and more abstract information from the initial electrical signals. Finally, the visual image is represented as a collection of contours and attributes.

This description is not sufficiently detailed to explain how we recognise a chair or a friend's face, but it is the beginning of an understanding of the hierarchical organisation and the complexity of the nervous system.

1.3.4 A Plastic System

Experiments with Cats

A number of kittens were raised in the dark for the first two weeks of their lives. Subsequently, they were exposed for five hours per day for a period of five months to a background consisting of black and white lines, some kittens to horizontal lines and some to vertical lines. Following this upbringing the kittens showed significant anomalies in their behaviour. Their movements were awkward and jerky, and whenever they found themselves in the presence of long objects, they only reacted if these objects had the same orientation as the lines amongst which they were brought up. Finally, electrical investigations showed that certain brain cells in these kittens were completely inactive.

These observations show that cats are born with a collection of brain cells which have no dedicated purposes. During the development of the cat, this collection can become sensitive to certain features of the environment. If these features are missing, certain cells become frozen and can never be subsequently used.

Memory and Learning

Sensory deprivation shows that a significant changes can occur in the anatomy of that part of the nervous system connected to an organ whose sense is deprived. This modification only takes place when the deprivation is carried out on a young individual, not when an adult is deprived.

More generally, this leads to the work of A. Danchin, described in [Del], on postnatal changes in nerve systems.

Recent research in electrochemistry suggests the following theory of the evolution of the nervous system: the growth of a particular nervous system follows a hereditary programme. At birth, the nervous system is defined by a network of neurons with a full set of connections, by the way in which each class of neuron functions and by the potential for change in synapses. All of these elements are under genetic control. The subsequent development of the nervous system is due to the interaction between the external environment and the genetic programme.

This development takes place by changes in synapses, some of which degenerate and some stabilise in a more or less reversible manner.

The idea of a 'synaptic' mechanism of coupling cells was proposed by Hebb in 1949.

Hebb's rule states:

> when a cell A excites cell B by its axon and when in a repetitive and persistent manner it participates in the firing of B, a process of growth or of changing metabolism takes place in one or in both cells such that the effectiveness of cell A in stimulating and impulsing cell B, is increased with respect to all other cells which can have this effect.

This suggests that the change in a synapse depends upon the exchanges of information between the two neurons connected by this synapse. This relates well to the theory that the evolution of the nervous system is due to the interaction between the environment and the genetic programme.

In summary, the development of a network takes place by means of a selective mechanism which imprints an image of the environment onto the network. At the biochemical level, learning and memory development can be characterised simply by changes in the connections between neurons.

The Electrochemical Model of Learning

The functional mechanisms of a neuron were explained in section 1.2.1. A hypothesis due to Changeux and Danchin, originating in their experimental work states that

> a synapse stabilises in a manner determined by the change in the molecular properties of the post-synaptic receptors (called neuroreceptors earlier).

To explain this learning process, consider a neuroreceptor which can exist in three different states: an unstable state (state U) in which it can diffuse freely, and in which it has little tendency to aggregate, a stable state (state S) in which it is incapable of diffusing but has a tendency to aggregate, and a degenerate state (state D) in which it does not permit the transfer of nervous impulses.

The neuroreceptor can change state in one of three different manners:

o type 1: $U \to S$
o type 2: $U \to D$
o type 3: $S \to U$

The neuroreceptor will achieve a final, stable state which depends on the full history of the signals which traverse the synapse containing this neuroreceptor.

Neuroreceptors are distributed throughout all of the branches of the nerve cell. If a particular synapse is traversed by a number of signals, a clump of neuroreceptors is formed there. This takes place thanks to the transformation of neuroreceptors from state U to state S. If the synapse is not stimulated, or is rarely stimulated by electrical signals, the type 2 and type 3 changes in neuroreceptors take place. In the case of a synapse which is never used, the neuroreceptors are all transformed by type 2 changes and the life of the neuroreceptors is finished.

This theory gives an interesting interpretation to the function of dreaming.

The adult nervous system, which is not continuously creating new connections, needs a special mechanism to keep a minimum level of operations active in order to prevent the entire network from degenerating. Dreams, autonomous ways of stimulating certain parts of the brain, are examples of this activity.

Conclusion

The post-natal development of the nervous system is characterised by four aspects: the initial state (or genetic framework) of a redundant system with fixed functional and evolutionary mechanisms, secondly, the development of connections within this network, third, the interaction between the external world and the network, and finally, its selective mechanism.

The mechanisms described above form the beginnings of a chemical theory of learning and memory. Learning can be defined as the acquisition of stable associations, or 'all relatively long-term modification in behaviour that can be attributed to the sensory inputs of the organism' (see [Del]); memory can be defined as the gathering and recalling of these properties or modifications.

These results seem to show that learning is a complex mixture of innate constraints and acquired experiences. Explaining memory in these simple terms is more difficult.

It is known that short-term memory is implemented by natural bioelectrical mechanisms, but the exact mechanisms of long-term memory are not presently well understood, nor are those of memory recall (see [Chap]).

A dominant idea in neurobiology is that of storing information in the macromolecules in the brain, either in proteins or in RNA, an idea whose origins date back to the discovery of the storage of genetic codes in DNA molecules. It is therefore tempting to establish an analogy between the ways that our innate and our acquired memories are stored.

1.4 Summary

The preceding material can be summarised under the headings biological or functional characterisations of the brain.

1.4.1 Biological Characterisation

A biological characterisation of the brain can be made at a very simple level by the description of its constituent parts, its architecture, its function, and its development.

The constituent parts of the brain are the neurons and its architecture is the manner in which these neurons are connected one to another. The brain function involves the study of the operation of neurons and of their interconnections, and describing the brain's development introduces the problems of memory and learning.

Investigations in these areas are part of neuroanatomy.

1.4.2   Functional Description of the Brain

The brain is characterised by its role within the organism, namely that of the central command system. This means that it needs to possess information, to be capable of processing this information and, finally, to direct the actions of the organism which shelters it.

2 Neural Models

Following the neuroanatomical observations and neurophysiology in chapter 1, this chapter is concerned with the most general models of networks of neurons that have been proposed. Although this part is largely theoretical, it considers one concrete example, the perceptron, which was the first serious attempt to simulate networks of neurons.

2.1 A Synthetic Neuron

2.1.1 The Model of McCulloch and Pitts

The first modelling of neurons dates back to the 1940s and was carried out by Mc-Culloch and Pitts. Drawing on their work on biological neurons, they proposed the following model: a synthetic neuron forms a weighted sum of the action potentials which arrive at it (each one of these potentials is a numeric value which represents the state of the neuron which has emitted it) and then activates itself depending on the value of this weighted sum. If this sum exceeds a certain threshold, the neuron is activated and transmits a response (in the form of an action potential) of which the value is the value of its activation. If the neuron is not activated, it transmits nothing.

This synthetic neuron is a boolean automata, that is, its inputs and outputs are boolean values.

We write:

o $(e_i)_{i=1,n}$ are the inputs to the synthetic neuron
o S its output
o β its threshold
o W_i its weights
o f is its threshold function, shown in figure 2.1:

$$f(x) = 1 \text{ if } x > \beta; f(x) = 0 \text{ otherwise}$$

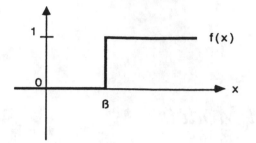

Figure 2.1   Threshold function

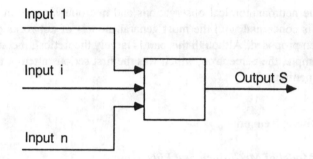

Figure 2.2   Neuron model

The operation of the complete synthetic neuron shown in figure 2.2 is given by:

$$S = f \left(\sum_{i=1,n} W_i e_i \right)$$

2.1.2   General Model

More generally, following [McCl] and [Fog], a synthetic neuron may be defined by the following five elements:

- o   the nature of its inputs;
- o   the input function, defining the preprocessing carried out on its inputs;
- o   the activation function (or state) of the neuron defining its internal state as a total of its inputs;
- o   the output function which determines the output of a neuron as a function of its activation state;
- o   the nature of the output of the neuron.

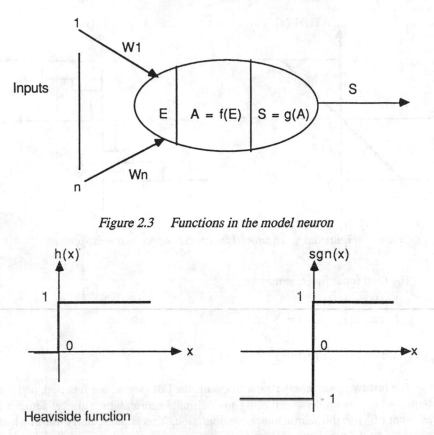

Figure 2.3   Functions in the model neuron

Heaviside function

Sign function

Figure 2.4   Heaviside and sign functions

We adopt the following notation:

o $(e_i)_{i=1,n}$ are the inputs;
o h is the overall input function;
o f is the activation function;
o g is the output function;
o $E = h(e_1, ..., e_n)$ is the total input;
o $A = f(E)$ is the state of the neuron (see figure 2.3);
o $S = g(A)$ is the neuron output.

The neuron inputs may be binary, with values of $(-1, +1)$ or $(0, 1)$, or they may be continuous, or real numbers.

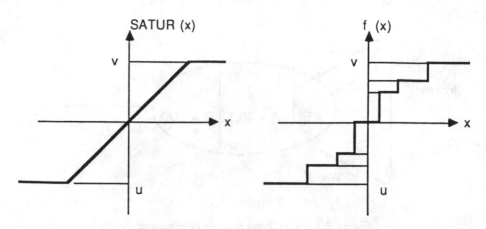

Figure 2.5   Threshold functions: single and multiple

The total input function may be

o boolean

o linear: $h(e_1, \ldots, e_n) = \sum_{i=1,n} W_i e_i$

o affine: $h(e_1, \ldots, e_n) = \sum_{i=1,n} W_i e_i - a$

The last two cases are the most frequent: the last is an affine function, and the term '−*a*' can be implemented using an additional neuron which always furnishes an input of −1 to the neuron under consideration. This is particularly useful when considering the problems of learning using activation functions with thresholds.

Alternatively, *h* may be a polynomial function of degree 2 or greater.

The activation function *f* may be a binary function with a threshold. In this case, *h* is arranged so that the Heaviside or sign functions, shown in figure 2.4, may be used. Alternatively, *f* may be a linear function with thresholds or with multiple steps, shown in figure 2.5.

The linear threshold function is known as SATUR:

$$\begin{aligned}
\text{SATUR}(x) \quad &= x \quad \text{if } u \leq x \leq v \\
&= u \quad \text{if } x < u \;\bullet \\
&= v \quad \text{if } x > v
\end{aligned}$$

Secondly, *f* may be a sigmoid function, shown in in figure 2.6:

$$f(x) = a\frac{(e^{kx} - 1)}{(e^{kx} + 1)}$$

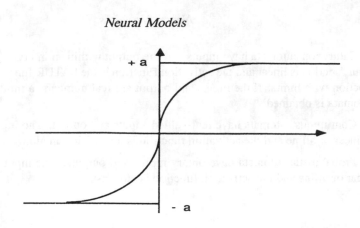

Figure 2.6   Sigmoid function

Alternatively, f may be a stochastic function: $f(x) = 1$ with the probability $1/(1+\exp(-\frac{x}{T}))$, or zero otherwise. T is a parameter called temperature: as T tends towards zero the function tends towards the threshold function.

Any other function may be used for f, but it is generally chosen to be monotonic and odd.

In general, the output function g is defined to be the identity function. In other words, the output of the neuron is made identical to its activation level.

$$S = f(E) = A$$

2.1.3   Common Cases

Six different models are most frequently encountered: boolean, threshold, linear, saturation, continuous, and probabilistic.

In the boolean device, inputs and the output are booleans. The output is a boolean function of the inputs.

The threshold device has an binary output whilst the inputs may be binary or continuous. The total input function is affine, and the activation function f is either the sign or the Heaviside function.

$$S = f\left(\sum_{i=1,n} W_i e_i - a\right)$$

Linear automata have inputs and outputs which are continuous functions. The input function is linear and the output function is the identity function.

$$S = \sum_{i=1,n} W_i e_i$$

Saturation automata have inputs and the output within an interval (U, V). The input function is linear and the activation function is the SATUR function, a linear function with limits. If the inputs and output are real numbers, a multi-threshold automata is obtained.

Continuous automata have real-valued inputs and output. The input function is linear or affine and the activation function is a sigmoid function.

Probabilistic automata have binary inputs and outputs. The input function is linear or affine and the activation function is stochastic.

2.2   The Structure of Connections

2.2.1   *The General Case*

Many different connection structures may be used. Biological studies of the brain have shown that the number of connections is enormous: for example, researchers have shown that the cortex is divided into a number of different layers. In one layer alone the number of interactions between neurons is large but the neurons in one layer are also connected to other layers, giving a total system whose complexity is almost unimaginable.

In general, the architecture of artificial neural networks may specify total connectivity (all the neurons are connected to all others) or local connectivity, in which neurons are only connected to their nearest neighbours. It is common to use networks with a regular connection structure to facilitate their implementations.

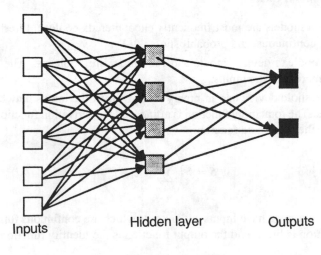

Inputs   Hidden layer   Outputs

Figure 2.7   Multilayer network

2.2.2 Two Classical Models

Layered Networks

The study of the visual system suggests that the nervous system is organised as successive layers of nerve cells. Signals arrive at sensory cells and are processed by an intermediate system of neurons, which have a complex interconnection including loops, before arriving at motor cells which perform some response.

Although this system, shown in figure 2.7, is simplified, it is already very complex to simulate if the fully connected structure in the part of the model that processes the signal is preserved.

For this reason, an alternative network structure with layers is frequently used, in which neurons that belong to a particular layer are not connected to each other. Each layer receives signals only from the previous layer and transmits results to the following layer. (See [McCl] and [Fog])

The two outermost layers correspond in one case to the layer which receives inputs from the external world and in the other to the layer which outputs the results of processing. The intermediate layers are called hidden layers and they may vary in number.

Fully Connected Networks

In these networks, each cell is connected to every other cell, including itself, as appears in figure 2.8.

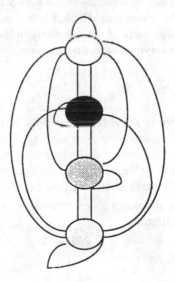

Figure 2.8   Fully connected network

The value of this model is not so much that it is derived from biological evidence, as was the case for layered networks, but the fact that it corresponds to the 'spin-glass' models of phase transitions which have been extensively studied by physicists.

This analogy enabled researchers to use all of the formalism of statistical mechanics and contributed to a rebirth of interest of the study of neural networks in the 1980s (see [Ami], [Per1] and [Per2]).

2.3   State Dynamics

One field of neural network study is the dynamics of states: the evolution of the states of different neurons in a network. It tries to determine the existence of stable states or stable cycles either of individual cells, of groups of cells or for the network as a whole (see [Ami], [Per1] and [Per2]).

Interest in this study area comes from the fact that when certain stimuli are presented to the brain, processing of the signals transmitted to the nerve cells generates a brain response characterised by an observable behaviour pattern. It is possible to describe stable relationships between certain stimuli and their responses, giving rise to the idea that the nervous system reaches stable configurations associated with its different inputs.

It is tempting, then, to look for associative properties in synthetic networks of neurons and, in particular, to investigate whether they have the same immunity to noise as is found in the networks of the brain.

Another step is to consider an artificial neural network as an autonomous system, to let it evolve, and to investigate whether it is capable of stabilising itself. This idea is motivated by the study of the autonomy of living systems rather than the previous goal, that of studying associative systems.

2.4   Connection Dynamics

In a synthetic neural network, the different neurons interact with one other by means of connections representing the synapses, as discussed in chapter 1. As described there, synapses can perform different roles: they may be inhibitors or excitors. In order to model this function, each connection between two artificial neurons may have a weight attached, to affect the transmitted signal.

The study of connection dynamics concerns networks whose connection weights vary during the network's lifetime.

2.4.1   The Cybernetic Model

The cybernetic model (see [Del]) is based upon the model of electrochemical evolution described in the previous chapter. It is characterised by an initial state in which the network is maximally connected, by the function of the artificial neurons and by a rule that governs the evolution of the connections. In this model, each artificial synapse can change between four states, N, U, D and S.

N is the non-existent state which precedes the functional creation of the network, U is an unstable state, D is a degenerate state, and S is a stable state. Changes at synapses can take place in the following manner. They pass from state N to state U when a fully connected network is created. The transition from state U to state D takes place by irreversible regression, and that between states U and S by reversible or irreversible stabilisation. The changes in the synapse depend on information which the neuron receives during the course of learning by means of the synapse.

The problem of cybernetics is to find out whether the network can reach a final state at the end of some finite time, given a particular environment and an evolutionary programme (in other words, knowing the way in which neurons function and the evolutionary rules that govern changes in the synapses as a function of their activity).

2.4.2 The Hebb Rule

As was seen in the study of the biological foundations, the Hebb rule is the primary evolutionary mechanism proposed for synapses. In artificial neural networks its interpretation is as follows: if two connected neurons are activated at the same moment, the connection between them is reinforced. In all other cases, the connection is not modified.

Following the conventions shown in figure 2.9, the Hebb rule gives the effect shown in figure 2.10. This reflects the fact that when the connection between two cells is very strong, when the emitting cell is activated, the receiving cell is also activated. For this reason, it is necessary to increase the weight of this particular connection during the learning stage, in order to set up this connection. On the other hand, if the emitting cell is activated without the receiving cell, or if the

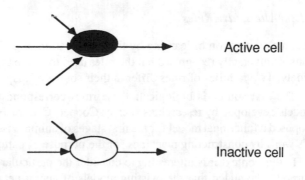

Active cell

Inactive cell

Figure 2.9   Active and inactive neurons

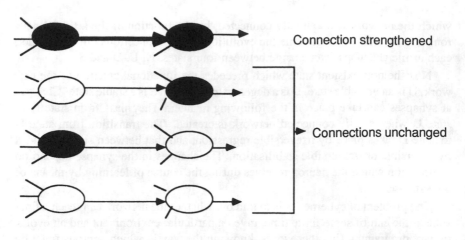

Figure 2.10   The Hebb rule in operation

receiving cell is activated without the emitting cell being active, this reflects the fact that the connection between these two particular cells is not dominant in the behaviour of the receptor cell. In these cases, it is necessary to leave a small weight on this connection during the learning phase.

The weight of the connection between neuron i and neuron j at time t is written $W_{ij}(t)$.

Imagine that the network is subjected to a stimulus between times t and $t + \delta t$; this stimulus causes the activation, A_i of neuron i, and the activation A_j of neuron j.

Furthermore, imagine that A_i and A_j are booleans (activations may take values in the range $(0, 1)$ or $(-1, +1)$; these are equivalent). The Hebb rule gives:

$$W_{ij}(t + \delta t) = W_{ij}t + \mu A_i A_j$$

In this equation, μ ($\mu > 0$) is a parameter giving the strength of learning.

2.4.3   Alternative Rules

The implementation of learning by the modification of weights between connections is universally recognised but the rules used to arrive at this modification vary widely. Two families of rules differ in their source of inspiration.

The first source is biological: these rules correspond to Hebb's rule and to models developed by researchers such as Cooper [Coo] or Fukushima [Fuk1] who proposed a functional model for the first stages of animal visual systems, extending this work by constructing machines for the purpose of pattern recognition.

In this context it is interesting to consider the particular contributions of Yves Burnod, who stated that the existing models of neural networks did not, in general, take account of the significant diversity which exists between the operation, connectivity and capacity for learning of different neurons. Furthermore, recent research work has revealed the existence of a modular architecture in the cerebral cortex whose basic unit, the cortical column, integrates the functioning of about 100 neurons. From the point of view of simulation, these columns have an advantage over neurons of having a common functional mechanism. They acquire their specific function by the type of inputs which they process.

Burnod proposed an operational model of the cortex based on real functional modules of cortical columns. This model has the potential to provide an intermediate solution between artificial neural networks, used to simulate the fundamental cognitive actions of the brain, and artificial intelligence, which simulates the higher cognitive activities of mankind such as reasoning.

The second source of rules for learning is mathematical. When constructing a network of neurons, along the lines suggested previously, the user is trying to get the network to perform a certain function, to recognise characters, for example, or to store information.

An alternative view is to regard the network as a transfer function between the inputs presented to it and its outputs. The difficult part is to characterise this transfer function well.

This step has led to models such as that of the perceptron and algorithms such as back-propagation, or the projection rule. These algorithms are based on minimisation of cost functions or on techniques of linear algebra (see [McCl] and [Cun]).

A number of other types of rules could be described here, but before doing so, it is appropriate to stress the importance of the back-propagation rule, introduced in the next chapter.

2.5 Functioning of the Models

2.5.1 Initial State

The initial state of the network may either be random or the input cells may be preset, other cells being either random or preset.

2.5.2 Operation

The first hypothesis made is that time is discrete, each time step being marked by a clock tick. Two principal modes of functioning are parallel and serial: in parallel mode, each neuron calculates its new activation state and its output at each clock tick, and transmits it to the neurons to which it is connected. This calculation is made as a function of each neuron's input after the previous clock tick.

In sequential mode, each clock tick causes one neuron only to calculate its new activation level and output, and to transmit this to its connected neurons. Again, this calculation is made as a function of its input at the previous clock tick.

Sequential mode may follow a cyclic list of neurons or may randomly choose, at each clock tick, which neuron will execute this procedure.

Hybrid modes may be constructed from different combinations of these two simple modes.

2.6   The Perceptron

2.6.1   *Origins and General Organisation*

Following the research of McCulloch and Pitts, who defined a synthetic neuron, and that of Hebb, who provided an explanation of the contribution of synapses to the process of learning, researchers were faced with the problem of explaining the functionality of the brain by reference to its structure.

In the late 1950s, neurobiology could not deploy the modern tools of electro-chemistry to study the structures of the brain. A number of researchers set out to use the models of neurons and the mechanisms of synapses to simulate networks of neurons. They hoped that, constructing these networks in accordance with biological constraints, the models might exhibit behaviour close to that of the brain and could thus shed light on the brain's operation.

The first concrete model was the perceptron, proposed by Rosenblatt in [Ros1]: the model appears in figure 2.11.

This model had a number of characteristics. It was specified in sufficiently precise terms to enable the performance claimed for it to be tested; it was sufficiently complex to give the hope of interesting behaviour, while being sufficiently simple to enable its performance to be predicted and analysed. Finally, and most importantly, its description was in agreement with biological reality.

A perceptron comprises three principal elements. The first is a retina composed of cells on which the stimulus is input. In the majority of perceptron models, these cells react in an all-or-nothing manner, but they might alternatively provide a response varying according to the intensity of the stimulus.

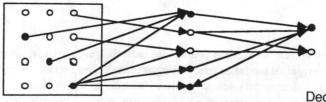

Retina   Associative cells   Decision cells

Figure 2.11   The perceptron

The perceptron also contains a layer of associative cells. Each one of these may be connected to cells of the retina, to other associative cells and to decision cells described below. An associative cell sums the impulses which arrive from cells to which it is connected. Again, in general, these cells follow an all-or-nothing law, comparing the effective sum of inputs to a threshold. Alternatively, they may respond in a continuous manner. The direction of connections between the layers is from the retina to the associative cells.

Lastly, the perceptron contains a layer of decision cells. These represent the output of the perceptron and operate in the same manner as associative cells, receiving their input from associative cells or from other decision cells. In the general perceptron model, connections between associative cells and decision cells can be made in both directions, permitting feedback to the network from its output.

To enable the evolution of the network, following the principles described by Hebb, each connection between associative cells and decision cells has an associated weight which may vary during the network's lifetime.

2.6.2 The Simple Perceptron

To simplify the study of the behaviour of a perceptron, it is common to use a more limited perceptron than that defined by the general model (see [Cun]).

In the simple case, binary output values, zero or one, are produced by all cells: retina cells, associative cells and decision cells. Furthermore, the functions implemented by the associative cells are binary functions and the decision cells are threshold gates. The final simplification is that no connections are permitted between two associative cells or two decision cells. This means that connections between associative cells and decision cells are in a single direction from associative to decision cells.

The simple perceptron model has only one layer of modifiable weights between the associative cells and the decision cell.

Considering the behaviour of such a system, it is interesting to investigate whether it is capable of implementing some functions of the brain. A perceptron system like this can be used to try to recognise shapes, presented to it on its retina. If a single decision cell is used, this may respond when the shape presented to the perceptron corresponds to the form which it recognises, and fail to respond in all other cases.

Learning in the perceptron model can take place using the Hebb rule and by modifying the weights on connections.

2.6.3 The Perceptron Rule

The perceptron learns by means of a supervised learning process which proceeds by correcting errors. This process is introduced using an intuitive explanation.

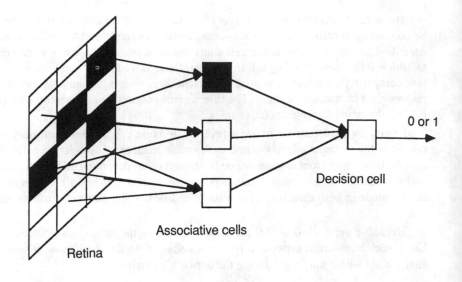

Figure 2.12   A 2-dimensional perceptron

Suppose that during training, a particular shape is presented to the retina of the perceptron and that the desired response at the decision cell is D. Using the notation introduced previously, we have an actual output S at the decision cell. This gives rise to four different cases:

o D = 1 and S = 1

o D = 0 and S = 0

o D = 0 and S = 1

o D = 1 and S = 0

In the two first cases, the desired actual responses are the same: no change to the weights is necessary.

In the third case the weighted sum of the inputs of the decision cell is above the threshold when it should be below, and it is therefore necessary to decrease the weights with positive values and increase the negative weights. For the fourth case we need to apply an inverse set of changes.

The hope is that, iterating this process over all possible inputs will give rise to a convergent process.

Using this notation, the rule of the perceptron is thus:

$$W_i \rightarrow W_i + k(d - s)e_i, \text{ with } k > 0$$

If $d = s$ the weights are not modified; if $(d - s) = 1$, W_i becomes $W_i + ke_i$.

In fact it is possible to show that if a solution exists, that is if there is a set of weights that can discriminate in the desired manner, then the procedure shown above is convergent.

One problem remains: to determine in what cases a solution exists.

2.6.4   Limitations of the Perceptron

It may be shown that a perceptr n of the type described can calculate any boolean function. This proof is simple: any boolean function can be decomposed into a sum of products. The products can be implemented on the first layer, using the associative cells, and the sum performed with the decision cell.

This result led Minsky and Papert of MIT to investigate how complex a perceptron needed to be to calculate a given boolean function (see [Min]). This introduces a further design choice: the complexity of the associative cells. These may have a limited number of inputs; they could be restricted to take their inputs from a particular area of the retina or their total number could simply be limited.

These two researchers proved a number of theorems about the limitations of perceptrons. These limitations caused a number of researchers to abandon this path and to divert their attention to problems in artificial intelligence, which seemed a more promising domain at the time.

One of the limitations that they proved was that a perceptron with a limited diameter could not recognise if a figure was simply connected. (A perceptron with limited diameter is a perceptron constructed in such a way that each associative cell is connected to cells on the retina which all lie within a maximum fixed distance D. This type of perceptron is also known as a perceptron with a limited field.) An intuitive version of their proof is given below.

Suppose that a perceptron with limited field is capable of recognising forms that are simply connected; restrict each associative cell to be connected only to cells on the retina that are situated in squares less than M cells wide. Consider figures 2.13 to 2.16, in which the lengths are greater than M cells.

Figure 2.13   Shape A

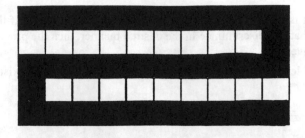

Figure 2.14   Shape B

Figure 2.15   Shape C

The associative cells may be divided into three categories: those which are connected to at least one cell at the left-hand side of the retina are type 1 cells, those connected to at least one right-hand cell of the retina are type 2, and those which are connected to neither left- nor right-hand cells are type 3.

Consider figure 2,13. If the response of the perceptron is positive, it is wrong. If the response of the perceptron is negative, call the weighted sum of the outputs of type 1 associative cells L, the sum of type 2 cells R and those of type 3, C. We deduce that the decision cell performs the weighted sum $C + L + B$. Because the response is negative, this sum is less than the threshold of the decision cell:

$$(C + R + L) < \beta$$

Figure 2.16   Shape D

Now consider figure 2.14. The only difference from figure 2.13 is in cells of type 1, and the sum L becomes L'. As the perceptron must respond positively in this case, it is necessary that the new weighted sum is greater than the threshold of the decision cell and therefore,

$$(C + R + L') > \beta \Rightarrow (L' > L)$$

Consider figure 2.15. Using similar reasoning, replacing type 1 by type 2 cells,

$$(C + R' + L) > \beta \Rightarrow (R' > R)$$

Finally, consider figure 2.16. Here the right-hand border is the same as that in figure 2.15 and the left-hand border is the same as in figure 2.14 and therefore the weighted sum becomes $(C + R' + L')$.

The previous relations give rise to

$$(C + R' + L') > \beta$$

The perceptron must therefore respond positively; it is therefore mistaken.

This argument demonstrates that a perceptron with a limited field cannot recognise connected shapes.

Minsky and Papert also demonstrated other limitations of the perceptron, such as the fact that it cannot implement the parity function if the associative cells are not connected to all of the input cells.

2.6.5 Summary

The perceptron was the first serious attempt to simulate networks of neurons. Inspired by the study of the brain, the model proved too simple, not capable of withstanding mathematical analysis. More complex models have been developed since, due to more recent developments in neurobiology and to the application of more powerful theoretical tools such as back-propagation and results of statistical physics.

Nevertheless, perceptrons showed that artificial neural networks could implement certain of the functions of the brain, even if these remained at a very limited level.

3 *Multi-layer Neural Networks*

This chapter describes the growth of multi-layer models of neural networks. The back-propagation algorithm, representing a mathematical solution to the problems encountered by the perceptron model, is then introduced. Back-propagation is probably the most widely used model today, permitting the best results to be obtained in many different applications.

3.1 Associative Networks and Pattern Recognition

Layered neural networks, introduced in the previous chapter in the context of the perceptron, are described below.

Layered networks involve a set of input cells connected to a collection of output cells by means of one or more layers of modifiable intermediate connections. The most natural use of this architecture is to implement associativity by associating an input shape, pattern, the representation of a concept or a situation, with another item, either of the same kind or totally different. For this reason, networks with multiple layers are described as associative networks.

Pattern recognition is the primary use of this mechanism. Pattern recognition is a popular application in that it enables the full set of human perceptions to be acquired by a machine.

Classically, pattern recognition is divided into a number of different stages whose relative importance varies depending on the sense being simulated and the method in use. In the context of vision, the different stages are: acquisition, concerned with digitising the data coming from a sensor such as a camera, scanner or a radar detector, localising, which involves extracting the object from its background, and representation which is finding a set of significant features on the object. The object is then represented by a real number, a word within a grammar, a graph or any element from a set of representations. The final stage, the decision stage, consists of dividing the set of object representations into a number of classes. For example, each class may contain the set of elements representing identical objects. In the decision stage, the class containing the current object is identified.

The last two phases, representation and decision, are the associative phases. The distinction between the two is poorly defined and varies depending on the problem in question. In character recognition, for example, it is possible to suppress the representation phase and proceed directly to a classification of the digitised image. The representation phase can be reduced to pre-processing in order to eliminate some noise. Alternatively, the representation phase might operate by describing the character's contours. Layered neural networks can play a part in each of these phases.

For example, the first applications envisaged for the perceptron were to use it as an adaptive classifier. Its learning rule allowed it to determine automatically a linear partition of the representation space, if one existed.

Associative neural networks allow many varied problems to be solved, not just the problem of pattern recognition. They have a learning behaviour which exhibits some interesting and promising properties.

3.2 Single-layer Associative Networks

3.2.1 The Perceptron and Linear Separability

The Perceptron Revisited

A perceptron consist of three elements, a retina of input cells, a layer of associative cells, and a decision cell. The only layer with modifiable connections is that which connects the associative cells to the decision cells. We therefore consider a simplified network obtained by omitting those components of the perceptron in advance of the associative cells.

The input cells of the simplified system are the associative cells of the previous system. This simplification is justified by the fact that the associative cells of a perceptron perform only a pre-processing operation and the essential classification work is carried out by the decision cell.

This decision cell permits a set of examples presented at the input to be partitioned into two classes; the problem of partitioning into more than two classes can be resolved simply by providing multiple decision cells working in parallel on the same inputs. P decision cells allow a partition into 2^P classes.

No generality is lost, then, in limiting our study to one single decision cell, a linear threshold neuron connected to N input cells, as shown in figure 3.1.

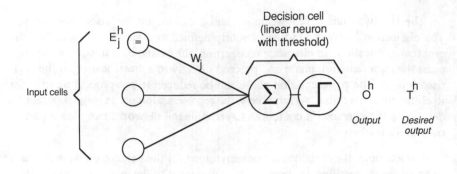

Figure 3.1   Linear threshold neuron

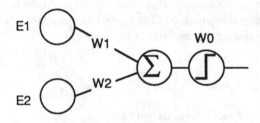

Figure 3.2   Two-input linear threshold neuron

We adopt the following notation:

E is the set of examples to be classified
E^h is one particular example
E^h_j is the value of the j-th element of the example E^h
W_j is the value of the weight connecting the j-th input cell to the decision cell
W_0 is the threshold of the decision cell
O^h is the output of the decision cell for the example h
$O^h = 1$ if $\displaystyle\sum_j W_j E^h_j \geq W_0$ and $O^h = 0$ otherwise.
T^h is the desired response for the example h

Linear Separation

A linear threshold neuron implements a partition of input vectors into two classes: the boundary between these classes is defined by the condition

$$\sum_j W_j E_j = W_0$$

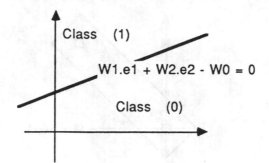

Figure 3.3   Linear separation into two classes

The border separating the two classes is thus a plane in hyperspace. This can be visualised very simply in two dimensions, as shown in figure 3.3.

Limitations

Neurons with thresholds have a strict limit on the power of their classification. It may be simply demonstrated that a threshold neuron cannot implement the boolean function XOR, no matter what its connections or its weights. Consider the table of the function, shown in figure 3.4. If a linear threshold neuron tries to implement this function it must respond zero for the two pairs (0,0) and (1,1) and must respond one for the two pairs (1,0) and (0,1). In other words, it needs linearly to separate the two classes {(0,0), (1, 1)} and {(1,0), (0,1).}

X	Y	XOR(X,Y)
1	1	0
1	0	1
0	1	1
0	0	0

Figure 3.4   Two-input XOR

Representing *X* and *Y* and the value of *XOR(X,Y)* on a graph (figure 3.5) shows this task to be impossible.

It is obvious that a number of other classification problems are similar in that they cannot be resolved by a linear separation.

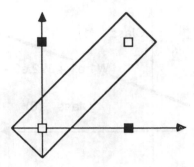

Figure 3.5   XOR in 2 dimensions

3.2.2   Widrow-Hoff Rule

The learning algorithm of the perceptron was described above by the sequence:

1. E^h, an example, is presented to the network
2. $\Delta^h = T^h - O^h$ is calculated
3. Each weight W_j is modified: $\Delta W_j = k\Delta^h E_j^h$

This method of learning needs a number of comments: first, the algorithm only converges if there is a solution to the problem in the form of linear separation. If this is not the case, the behaviour of the algorithm is not guaranteed and, in particular, it is not certain that it will find a solution even close to the problem.

Secondly, if there are a number of solutions, that is many different hyperspace planes can separate the two example classes, the quality of the solution found by the perceptron is unknown. The quality of the solution will affect the capacity of the perceptron to give accurate responses for new examples and affect its capacity for generalisation. Looking at figure 3.6, for example, the user will probably prefer solution (b) to (a).

Lastly, in certain problems it may be preferable to permit certain classification errors rather than insist on an exact solution based on cases which are too specific or possibly erroneous (due, for example, to errors in measurement). In figure 3.6 again, solution (c) seems, from this point of view, better than solution (d), even if it does contain two classification errors.

The learning rule proposed by Widrow and Hoff in 1960 (see [Wid]) addresses all of these criticisms and has a number of interesting features.

In the Widrow-Hoff rule, a distinction is made between the classification criterion and the learning rule. During classification the same linear thresholded element is used as in the perceptron, with an output of + 1 if the weighted sum of its inputs is positive or −1 otherwise.

The learning rule is modified, however. In the perceptron, the error signal used to calculate the modification of weights is equal to the difference between

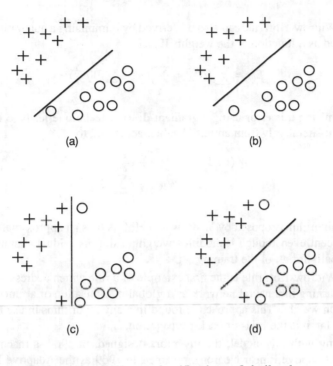

(a)   (b)

(c)   (d)

Figure 3.6   Different classifications of similar data

the weighted input sum after thresholding and the desired result. In the Widrow-Hoff rule the error signal is equal to the difference between the weighted sum of the inputs before thresholding and the desired output.

In other words, the Widrow-Hoff rule modifies connection weights when the weighted sum of the inputs of the neuron is not exactly equal to +1 or −1, even if the thresholded response is correct.

The different rules are:

$$\Delta^h = T^h - O^h \qquad \qquad perceptron\ rule$$
$$\Delta^h = T^h - \sum_j W_j E_j^h \quad Widrow\text{-}Hoff\ rule$$

In each rule, the weights are modified at each step using:

$$\Delta W_j = k\Delta^h E_j^h$$

Note that this rule does not strictly minimise the numbers of errors in classification even if a linear classification exists, particularly in the case where the two classes are represented in a very uneven manner. Rather than find a linear separation somewhere between the two training classes this rule allows a boundary (or plane in hyperspace) to be found which is the best possible, given the two classes.

The Widrow-Hoff rule can also be derived by minimising a quadratic equation, considered as a function of the weights $W_{j,j=1,n}$:

$$Err = \sum_h (\Delta^h)^2 = \sum_h (T^h - \sum_j W_j E_j^h)^2$$

Minimising this error using a gradient descent technique leads to modifying the weights iteratively from an initial value, according to:

$$\begin{aligned} W_j(t+1) &= W_j(t) + k\frac{\delta Err}{\delta W_j} \\ &= W_j(t) + k\sum_h \Delta^h E_j^h \end{aligned}$$

The algorithm proposed by Widrow and Hoff is thus an approximation to gradient descent even though it modifies weights using individual examples rather than globally for all of the training set.

The Widrow-Hoff rule is the first example of a rule which addresses the problem of learning in a neural network as a global minimisation of a function of the connection weight. This approach is found in many algorithms in use today and, in particular, it is the basis of back-propagation.

Starting with this model, the inventors designed, in 1960, a machine called Adaline (Adaptive Linear Neuron), renamed in 1969 as the Adaptive Linear Element Machine (see [Wid]). This machine implemented recognition of simple patterns, with 16 points, dividing the patterns into two classes.

3.2.3   Single-layer Networks: A General Framework

In this section we describe some variations on the single layer model of neural networks found in the literature. They all have two characteristics in common, the architecture of the network, a collection of input cells connected to a set of output cells by a layer of modifiable connections, and the calculation performed by each output cell which is a weighted sum of its inputs.

$$I_i = \sum_j W_{ij} O_j$$

The variants differ in the way that output cells calculate their activation level and in the way that the weights of intermediate cells are modified.

Activation of the Output Cells

Four principal models for output cell activation exist:

- o The linear model (Widrow-Hoff), in which the activation level (or output) of the output neuron is equal to its total input: $O_i = I_i$

o The threshold model (perceptron): $O_i = \text{sgn}(I_i)$
o The stochastic model, in which the output of a neuron is 1 with probability p :

$$p_{(O_i=1)} = 1/(1 + \exp(-I_i/T))$$

(T is a constant called the temperature; as T tends towards zero, the stochastic neuron tends towards the threshold neuron.)

o The continuous model, using a sigmoid function:

$$O_i = 1/(1 + \exp(-I_i/k))$$

The Learning Rule

As introduced in the previous chapter, the first learning rule was qualitatively formulated by Hebb in 1949; in outline, it acts by reinforcing the connection between two neurons every time that they are simultaneously activated. This rule may be quantified most simply using the formula:

$$\Delta W_{ij} = kO_iO_j$$

The assumptions are that learning is begun with all connection weights set to zero, and that for an example from the training set, the neurons in both the input *and* output layers are forced to their desired values before the variation on connection weights is calculated.

The total value of connection weights after the network has been shown a set p of training examples is:

$$W_{ij} = k \sum_{h=1,p} O_i^h O_j^h$$

This rule will be encountered again in chapter 4.

The other learning rule variant is based on the idea of progressively reducing the difference between the desired output and the actual output. This is the perceptron rule, or the Widrow-Hoff rule.

3.2.4 An Application

An interesting application is described in the paper 'On Learning Past Tenses of English Verbs' [Ru3].

This application demonstrates the ability of an associative network to generalise, using the problem of learning the past tenses of English verbs, both regular and irregular. The initial objective of the work was to show that single-layer associative networks could give an insight into speech learning processes in young children.

Studies carried out by psycholinguists have shown evidence of three distinct phases when children learning English as their mother tongue first encounter the past tense.

In the first phase, the child learns a small number of very common verbs, many of which are irregular. He makes very few errors in his use of the past tense, but it cannot be said that he distinguishes regular and irregular verbs: he has learned a number of independent pairs of (present, past) forms.

The child continues to learn more and more verbs, and the proportion of regular verbs increases. Now, it seems that the child develops an intuitive knowledge of rules for forming the past tense: he can conjugate new verbs in the past, and he starts to commit errors when using irregular verbs that he learned correctly in the first phase. This shows that he has developed the tendency to regularise.

In the third phase, the child learns to use both the rules and their exceptions, while continuing to regularise new verbs presented to him. These habits persist into adulthood.

Rumelhart and McClelland simulated this learning process on a single-layer neural network. The model they used was as follows: the inputs and outputs of the network were the verb in present and past tenses respectively. They used an encoding based on the phonetic characteristics of the verbs, proposed by Wickelgren [Wic]. Each verb was represented, in each tense, by 480 binary digits, each bit representing the presence or absence of a particular phonetic feature. The network operated following the Widrow-Hoff rule, and activation of output neurons were calculated according to the stochastic rule of section 3.2.2.

The full results of the simulation are described in [Ru3], but they showed a number of interesting features.

The model exhibited the three learning stages shown above. The model was initially trained with 10 very common verbs, each of which was presented 10 times. After this first training phase, the network gave good associative performance over these 10 verbs. Subsequently, 410 further verbs were added to the training set and the full set of 420 verbs presented to the network 190 times. During the first 30 or so iterations, the network showed a strong tendency to regularise the irregular verbs, a tendency which diminished over the subsequent training, so that it gave correct responses over the full set of examples.

At the end of training, the network was capable of responding correctly to regular verbs which it had never learned. In addition, certain irregular verbs, in certain groups containing sub-regularities, were also correctly conjugated.

This study led its authors, Rumelhart and McClelland, to note the value of simulated neural networks in the modelling of cognitive processes.

Apart from this aspect of the work, some further observations can be made about this example. The network was capable of synthesising a conjugation rule from a number of examples. These rules, in the nature of English language, are fuzzy, difficult to derive, and contain numerous exceptions and sub-rules. The only work required to solve the problem using a neural network is to find a suitable representation; this enables the network to find a complete solution, which includes the capacity for generalisation.

3.2.5 The Limits of Single-layer Networks

The perceptron algorithm, implemented on a single-layer network, guarantees convergence to a solution whenever the problem is soluble. Unfortunately, the class of problems addressed is limited to the set of linearly separable problems, as described above.

Two points are worth mentioning:

o the proportion of linearly separable functions in the set of n-dimensioned boolean functions decreases exponentially with n;

o A linear threshold neural network of two layers is capable of calculating all boolean functions by implementing a sum-of-products, as seen in chapter 2.

To illustrate the second point, it is instructive to consider the XOR example again. The graphical representation of this problem in two dimensions, in figure 3.7, shows that the problem is not linearly separable.

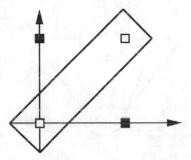

Figure 3.7   XOR in 2 dimensions

However, a revised problem, shown in the table in figure 3.8, may be considered. This is an extension of XOR into 3 dimensions (the third dimension is obtained by ANDing the first two). Figure 3.9 shows that a linear separation is possible.

$$
\begin{array}{ccccc}
0 & 0 & 0 & \rightarrow & 0 \\
0 & 1 & 0 & \rightarrow & 1 \\
1 & 0 & 0 & \rightarrow & 1 \\
1 & 1 & 1 & \rightarrow & 0 \\
\end{array}
$$

Figure 3.8   XOR - a 3 dimension solution

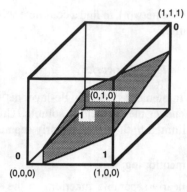

Figure 3.9   XOR - linear separation in 3 dimensions

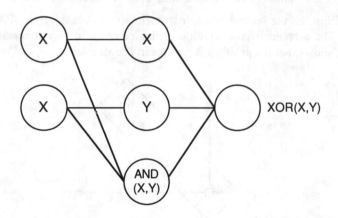

Figure 3.10   XOR - implementation in 2 layers

This shows that XOR is realisable with a network of linear threshold neurons with 3 layers, shown in figure 3.10.

This example shows the value of generalising the perceptron algorithm to form networks with more than one layer: this enables the resolution of any separation problem, be it linear or not. (The overall size of network necessary is not so simply defined!)

However, introducing extra layers introduces an additional conceptual difficulty.

The rules used previously to manipulate the connection weights rely on a supervised learning process: at each stage the desired output of each neuron is known. A 'teacher' guides the network at each stage of learning, indicating the correct result.

If a supplementary layer of neurons is introduced, between the input and output layers, how is the impact of modifying one of the intermediate weights upon the output to be assessed?

Put another way, how is the 'teacher' to know what outputs are required of the intermediate layer in the network?

3.2.6   The Credit Assignment Problem

The problem of weight adjustment in a multi-layer network is a particular case of the 'credit assignment problem', which appears in all learning systems, both natural and artificial.

For example, when a chess player loses a game, it is very difficult for him to learn the correct lessons from this defeat, except when he has made a flagrant error in the end-game. In particular, it is impossible to draw conclusions about the value of each of the individual moves that he played during the game.

In the case of neural networks with multiple layers of modifiable connections, the problem occurs in the following manner: how should the error signal, measured only at the network output, be used to modify each individual connection, which contributes only slightly, perhaps non-linearly, to the output?

This problem was quickly identified, and gave rise to a number of partial solutions, none of which was completely satisfactory until the development of 'back-propagation' in the early 1980s.

3.3   Back-propagation

3.3.1   Introduction

The learning rule now known as 'back-propagation' is a generalisation of the Widrow-Hoff rule for multi-layer networks. It was developed independently by two teams, one (Fogelman-Soulié, Gallinari and Le Cun) in France, the other (Rumelhart, Hinton and Williams) in the U.S.A.

The idea underpinning this algorithm, permitting the 'credit assignment' problem to be overcome, is the use of a differentiable function, such as a sigmoid, to replace the threshold function used in simple linear networks.

Mathematically, the algorithm uses the rules of compound differentiation, presenting no particular difficulties.

The algorithm relies on propagating an error signal from an output neuron backwards, through intermediate layers, towards the network input, in the same way that normal operation propagates the signal from input neurons, via intermediate layers, towards the output cells.

The neuron used is similar in nature to the perceptron cell: it applies an activation function to the weighted sum of its inputs. The activation function is a 'smoothed' form of the threshold function. A sigmoid function is most commonly used:

$$f(x) = \frac{1}{1 + e^x}$$

The network used has a number of layers: an input layer, corresponding to a retina, an output layer, corresponding to the decision, and some internal, or 'hidden' layers. These hidden layers will be shown later to represent hidden features of the problem. Each neuron is connected to all of the neurons in the next layer, by connections whose weight is given by variable real numbers.

Learning follows the same principles as the Widrow-Hoff rule. A training set is provided, containing a number of desired (input, output) pairs. At each stage, an example from the training set is presented to the input of the network. An actual output is calculated from the current network weights, proceeding in order from the input layer to the output layer. This phase is called the forward propagation, or relaxation, phase. Next, the total error (the sum of the squares of the errors on each output cell) is calculated. This error is then back-propagated through the network, giving rise to a modification of each connection weight. This process is repeated, by presenting each example from the training set in turn.

After a number of training sessions, if the error is below some particular threshold, the network can be regarded as having converged. Learning consists of minimising the squared error appearing on each output over the full set of training examples. By considering the error as a function of the weights, this minimisation is carried out by gradient descent, as in the case of the Widrow Hoff rule.

The essential difficulty in carrying out this descent in a multi-layered network, is being able to calculate the derivative of the squared error for a particular weight. The use of neurons with action function which is differentiable enables this problem to be overcome simply.

3.3.2 *Formalisation*

A formal presentation for the back-propagation algorithm appears below; further details appear in appendix A or in [Cun2], [Ru1] or [Ru2].

For an example in the training set, X represents the input vector and Y the desired output vector. If the network contains n input neurons and m output neurons, X and Y are given by:

$$X = (X_1, X_2, X_3, ..., X_n)$$
$$Y = (Y_1, Y_2, Y_3, ..., Y_m)$$

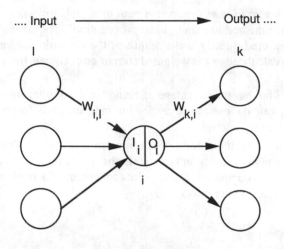

Figure 3.11   Back-propagation - notation

S is the output vector obtained when the input vector X has propagated through the whole network. The aim of back-propagation is to minimise the quadratic error between the desired and actual outputs, considering this error as a function of the connection weights.

$$E(W) = \sum_{i=1,m} (Y_i - S_i)^2$$

The rule for modifying the weights, when example X is presented for the k'th time is:

$$W_{ij}(k) = W_{ij}(k-1) - e(k)d_iO_j$$

where d_i is calculated step by step from the output layer to the input layer:

$$d_i = 2.(S_i - Y_i)f'(I_i) \quad \text{(output layer)}$$
$$d_i = \sum_h d_hW_{hi}f'(I_i) \quad \text{(hidden layers)}$$

The variable h ranges over the neurons to which neuron i is connected.

f is the sigmoid function of an individual neuron
f' is the derivative of f
O_j is the output of neuron j
I_i is the input of neuron i; $I_i = \sum_j W_{ij}O_j$

$e(k)$ is the step size at iteration k

This notation and the calculation is summarised in figure 3.11.

The error signal follows the reverse path of signals from the input of the network, giving the method its name, 'back-propagation'. The error signal for output neurons is measured directly at the output of the network; for internal cells, the error signal is calculated as the weighted sum of error signals from the subsequent layer.

This algorithm has the advantage of being local: in other words, the majority of the learning calculations can be carried out independently for each neuron, with a minimum of global control.

Locality in a learning algorithm is important for two reasons: to preserve a certain biological plausibility and to enable the use of implementations of the algorithm on parallel computers. Some points concerning the implementation of the algorithm are discussed in section 3.3.4.

3.3.3   Examples

Minsky and Papert, concluding their celebrated work *Perceptrons* [Min], predicted that the generalisation of associative networks to multi-layered architectures would not be especially fruitful. In particular, it seemed unlikely to them that an effective learning algorithm for such a network could be found. Since learning is such an obvious difficulty in multi-layer networks, it is interesting to show that back-propagation is capable of finding solutions to classic problems which are not linearly separable.

One classic problem is that of parity (see [Ru1]), consisting of determining if an N-bit word contains an even number of 1's. This problem is a generalisation of the XOR function.

One significant difficulty comes from the fact that very similar inputs (differing by only 1 bit) must give different outputs. This problem can be resolved without difficulty by a network containing three layers, a layer of n input neurons, an intermediate layer of n neurons, and one output neuron. The solution 'found' by the network in figure 3.12 is interesting, in that the neurons in the hidden layer implement a coding which depends simply on the number of units active in the input word. The first hidden neuron for example, is active if the input pattern contains at least one bit set and in general the n first neurons are active if there are at least n bits set in the input word. The hidden layers of neurons have thus implemented a count of the active bits on the first layer. It is very simple to decide the parity of the input word from this encoding.

Data Compression

A simple and original application of multi-layer neural networks using back-propagation is data compression; consider the network shown in figure 3.13.

During the learning stage the same vector (for example an image) is used as input and as the desired output of the network. If learning is carried out with a

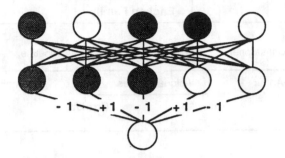

Figure 3.12 Solution to the parity problem

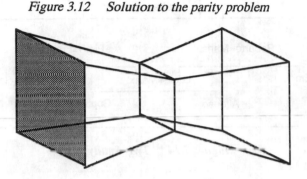

Figure 3.13 A network for data compression

certain number of images, the hidden layer of the network performs an encoding of the images presented at the input, since this layer is smaller than the input itself.

Binary encoders are a good simple way of illustrating this data compression. For example, constructing an 8 to 3 line encoder consists of making a network learn to associate an 8 bit word (with only 1 bit set) with itself, by passing it through a layer with only 3 bits. In some cases, the network will automatically implement a binary coding with 3 bits:

$$10000000 \rightarrow 111 \rightarrow 10000000$$
$$01000000 \rightarrow 110 \rightarrow 01000000$$

3.3.4 Hidden Representations

The use of hidden layers was a decisive step in the study of neural networks.

Multi-layer networks have a great deal of freedom in resolving the problems of classification or association. They are not restricted to finding a direct association between input and output, but they can use a set of intermediate variables to implement this association. The hidden layers can contain real internal representations of the problem; [Ru2] shows this in the context of back-propagation.

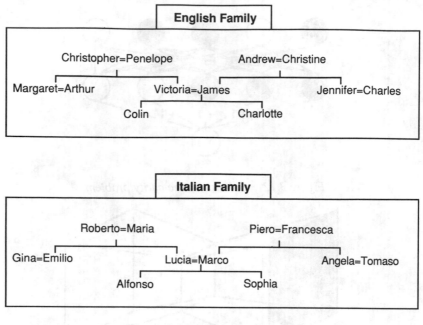

Figure 3.14   Two family trees

The back-propagation algorithm finds solutions to parity and data compression problems that demonstrate the interest of internal representations. After training, the hidden units often represent a characteristic of the training examples; sometimes this characteristic has a significance in the context of the overall problem.

A simple example illustrates the notion of internal representation. Hinton, in [Ru2], studied a network which was capable of memorising two families, one English, the other Italian, both having the same shape of family tree. The two trees appear in figure 3.14. The network was capable of answering questions about these family trees.

The examples are presented to the network in the form of associations, (*<person-1>*, *<relation>*) → *<person-2>*. There are 24 people in each tree and 12 relationships are possible: (father, mother, wife, husband, son, daughter, uncle, aunt, brother, sister, nephew and niece). The network had the following structure: each person was represented by one neuron in the group *person-1* and one in the group *person-2*. In the same way, each possible *relation* is represented by a neuron in the relation group. A diagram of the network appears as figure 3.15.

To train the network, to teach it, for example, that Jennifer is Colin's aunt, the neuron corresponding to 'Colin' is activated in the *person-1* group and the neuron corresponding to 'aunt' is activated in the *relation* group. At the output on the *person-2* group, it is necessary to activate the neurons corresponding to Jennifer and to Margaret, both of whom are Colin's aunts.

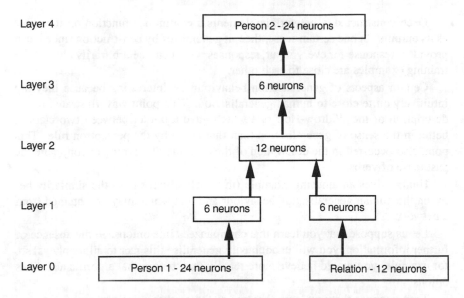

Figure 3.15   Network structure for family tree problem

Learning using the back-propagation algorithm converged after about 1500 presentations. The solution found by the network had a number of interesting properties; for example, examining the six neurons in layer 1 it was found that one of the neurons represented the nationality: it was active for an Italian and inactive for an English person. In the same way, another encoded the generation: it was very active for Christopher, Andrew and their Italian equivalents, less active for Margaret and Victoria, and almost inactive for Colin and Charlotte. A third neuron encoded the side of the family tree. It was highly active for one side of the tree (Andrew, Christine, James, Jennifer, Charles, Charlotte and their Italian equivalents) and inactive for the other.

The network had thus worked out a representation relevant to the problem, a representation which was not at all explicit in the encoding chosen for the inputs and outputs, since one unit was used for each person. It is apparent that this example is well chosen to illustrate these features; nevertheless, many modern studies have been made of the interpretation of hidden layers of a neural network trained by back-propagation on a certain problem. These hidden layers sometimes contain astute solutions to the problems.

Generalisation

The generalisation capacity of a neural network is its capacity to give a satisfactory response for an input which is not part of the set of examples on which it was trained.

Once constructed, a network implements a continuous function on its inputs as its outputs. In one certain sense, then, it generalises by construction since it can provide a response for every input, responses which can be arbitrarily close if the training examples are close to each other.

Certain aspects of generalisation behaviour are interesting because they are intuitively quite close to human generalisation. This point was illustrated in the description of the Widrow-Hoff rule which gave a border between two classes, better in the sense of generalisation than that given by the perceptron rule. This point also occurred in the description of the example of learning to conjugate the past tense of verbs.

Hinton gives an amusing example (in [Hin]) which shows the similarity between the human generalisation behaviour and that which may be obtained from a network.

Let us suppose that you learn that chimpanzees like onions. In the absence of further information, you will undoubtedly generalise this fact to all monkeys, so, for example, you would believe more readily than before that a gorilla also likes onions.

Then suppose that you learn that two or three other monkeys, orang-outangs, for example, and gibbons, do not like onions; this would give rise to the thought that this taste is specific to chimpanzees and you might revise your thoughts about gorillas.

When you learned the first piece of information about chimpanzees, you had no *a priori* reason to believe either that this information was true for all monkeys or was specific to chimpanzees. The information that you received later enabled you to relate the first fact to chimpanzees in particular, rather than to general characteristics common to all monkeys.

Consider a neural network in which we attempt to represent similar knowledge.

One might have, at the input, a certain number of characteristics, either qualitative (is capable of standing upright) or quantitative (height, weight) to describe any mammal, and at the output, we might have a bit which indicates if the animal enjoys eating onions.

If the network is taught that chimpanzees love onions, all of the connections which relate units representing chimpanzees to the unit representing onions will be incremented. The response from the network, presented with the representation of a gorilla at the input, will no doubt be high since the representation of the two monkeys is very similar.

If the network is taught subsequently that orang-outangs and gibbons do not like onions, the 'liking onions' feature will no longer be connected to the representation of all monkeys, but rather to a particular pattern for the representation of chimpanzees. If the network is now presented with the representation of a gorilla, it will give a response which is much less strong than previously.

More technically, the degree of generalisation possible is related to the quality of the classification boundaries set up by the network. These boundaries must not be too close to examples in the training set or cause instability between the different classes. Training for too long, for example, by forcing the output to reach a very small error over the training set, damages the network's capacity for generalisation, since the frontiers obtained by the network become very close to the examples that have been learned.

The capacity for generalisation is an essential feature of a classification system. We have seen that qualitatively at least, neural networks seem to have desirable properties from this point of view. More formal study of this point would need a quantitative definition of the capacity for generalisation; this lies outside the scope of this book.

3.3.5 Applications

Back-propagation has been studied and is used in a number of different application domains. The primary domain is pattern recognition in the classical sense, involving the simulation of human perceptions. Classic work has been done in the area of character recognition of both printed and hand-written characters. Speech processing has been investigated: 'NETTalk', from Sejnowski, is a neural network which performs voice synthesis and is capable of 'reading' a text. Interesting results are similarly being obtained in voice recognition.

The field of pattern recognition can be extended if it is noted that diagnosing illnesses or faults is a related problem. Golmard and Le Cun, for example, studied the application of back-propagation networks to the problem of diagnosing abdominal pains. They used 5,765 studies of illnesses, each case being described by 132 qualitative or quantitative symptoms, dividing the cases into two groups, one for training, and one for testing. They obtained of the order of 55 per cent correct diagnoses using the neural network, as against 44 per cent with a Bayesian classification. They note that a medical practitioner, in an emergency situation, gives a correct diagnosis in about 60 per cent of cases.

Games in which certain situations may be recognised are another potential application domain.

Back-propagation also provides solutions in the financial domain and any other area which involves a large number of parameters of different types in making a decision. Consider for example, authorisation of credit or of an overdraft by a bank. It is necessary to consider a client's profile, including his socioprofessional class, the average level of his balance, the number of overdrafts and amounts granted previously, and a number of other variables, both qualitative and quantitative, before making a decision about giving credit and its amount. An application along these lines has been successfully implemented by an American company.

These applications are described in more detail in chapter 6.

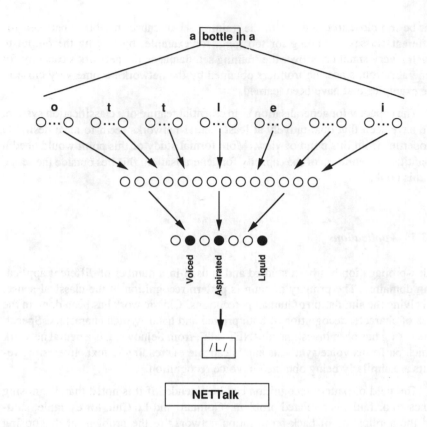

Figure 3.16   NETTalk

NETTalk

The problem of learning the conjugation in the past tense of English verbs both regular and irregular was described earlier. As in all the rules of language, the rules of pronunciation are vague and contain many exceptions: for example, in the phrase 'this is', the syllable 'is' is pronounced successively 'i s s' and 'i z'.

Nevertheless, it is possible to formalise these rules. DECTalk, an expert system developed by Digital Equipment Corporation, is capable of transforming a written English text into its phonetic representations and then pronouncing it using a voice synthesiser. This system took many years to develop, defining the rules and their exceptions.

NETTalk (see [Sej]) is a three-layer neural network, using back-propagation, capable of implementing the same function following a learning stage.

Consider the representation of the problem that was chosen and the architecture of the network which results, as summarised in figure 3.16.

A window of seven characters advances through the text, acting as the input to the first layer of the network, which outputs the phoneme corresponding to the central letter of the window. This method allows the network to take account of the context of an individual character when associating it with a phoneme. To represent the seven input characters, seven groups of 29 neurons are used: the alphabetic characters, space and punctuation are represented. A phoneme is represented by a combination of phonetic characteristics taken from a set of 26: the zone of vibration (lips or teeth), the type of phoneme (stop, nasal or fricative), the height of a vowel (high, intermediate or low), punctuation (silence, elision, pause, complete stop), and accentuation.

With a hidden layer of 80 neurons, NETTalk thus consists of around 300 neurons and 20,000 connections. The network was trained with isolated words and with continuous text. After 12 hours of learning, a 95% success rate was found on the learning data. With a new text, about 80% success was obtained. In each case the errors committed were quite close to the correct pronunciation. NETTalk is certainly not capable of managing subtle differences, which need a knowledge of syntactic or semantic information. A window of seven characters is completely insufficient for this and it would be difficult to improve the performance of NETTalk while keeping the same representation of the problem.

Sejnowski prepared recordings of the text 'read' by NETTalk at different stages in its learning process. These tapes are now widely known; they are very entertaining as NETTalk commits a number of errors which are strangely similar to those committed by young children.

3.3.6 Difficulties and Limitations

The back-propagation algorithm, in spite of having proved useful in a number of problems, still presents a certain range of difficulties which have not been resolved.

Network Architecture

There is no theoretical result nor even a satisfactory empirical rule suggesting how a network should be dimensioned to solve a particular problem. Should the network use one hidden layer or more? How many neurons should there be on the hidden layers? What is the relationship between the number of training examples, the number of classes to separate these examples into, and the overall size of the network?

Convergence

The minimisation problem that back-propagation attempts to solve is not a simple problem. The surface of the error function can contain features which obstruct the gradient descent technique, preventing the algorithm from converging, such as local minima plateaus, very shallow slopes and so on. There is no theoretical proof of the convergence of the algorithm, nor even a partial proof under particular, regular conditions. In most practical cases, however, the problem of local minima is rarely encountered. It is encountered much more frequently in artificial test cases. The most serious problem with the algorithm is usually the speed of its convergence.

In its original version, the algorithm contains a number of continuous parameters which it is difficult to control directly. These include, for example, the step of the gradient descent technique. It is clear that this parameter is of significant importance: if the step size is too small, for example, convergence of the entire network will take too many steps, while if the step size is too large, there is the risk of oscillation.

Calculation Time

The back-propagation algorithm, operating on significant problems, consumes large quantities of computing time.

In addition, no theoretical result relates the 'complexity' of a problem to the learning time that it needs. Such a result may possibly be obtained in the future, but if the learning time proves to be exponential as a function of the complexity of the problem, the result might strike a fatal blow to the algorithm itself.

Teaching Method

The teaching procedure may choose the order in which to present the training set to a neural network. We will discover later that this order can significantly affect the speed of learning. Normally, the method chosen is to present each example once, and to repeat a sequence containing each example. However, there are some cases in which it is necessary to present one or more examples several times during a training sequence, in order to achieve a satisfactory learning process.

A better understanding of these problems may be obtained by systematic experimentation with this algorithm. Unfortunately, one significant limitation is the calculation power that this would need. For large networks with perhaps 100,000 connections, this experimentation could only be carried out using the best possible tools, such as parallel or vector computers.

3.4 Development of the Back-propagation Model

The neural network model with multiple layers is the subject of much contemporary research, for a number of reasons. The association schema implemented by the back-propagation model and the principle of supervised learning is very simple and can be used in many different problems: the algorithm has shown its practical value in many different applications. The model itself is under investigation, as it is not completely satisfactory, having theoretical problems such as local minima, complexity, and practical difficulties with its use, and attempts are being made to refine it.

Some of these research directions are described below.

3.4.1 Back-propagation

The teams which invented back-propagation continue to improve the algorithm, both in the theoretical sense and in practical terms. Very few theoretical results about the algorithm have come to the authors' attention to date. One interesting research direction, which might give some quantitative measure of the quality of classifications obtained by a network, might be to compare the results of back-propagation learning with data analysis methods, such as principal component analysis or discriminant analysis. This comparison is quite natural in the sense that back-propagation is a method of minimising a squared error, the difficulty arising in the non-linearity of this method.

A number of workers are carrying out practical work with the aim of improving the convergence speed of the algorithm. Once the problem is stated as minimising the error as a function of connection weights, it is possible to use more effective methods, such as those arising from applied mathematics, than simple gradient descent. Two significant problems occur using this approach: firstly the methods may involve the use of approximations whose validity may be uncertain in this application, considering the form of the function to be minimised, and secondly, the local character of the original algorithm may be lost.

Other interesting work bears on the *a priori* adequacy of a particular network to tackle a specific problem. In pattern recognition, for example, it may be possible to construct a network in such a way as to use a certain structural regularity. Consider an input retina connected to a layer of cells. Each cell in this second layer gets its input, not from the full set of retinal cells, but only from a small neighbourhood (3 by 3 perhaps) in the retina. More and more successive layers may be added, constructed in the same way. Apart from reducing the number of connections considerably, which gives rise to a similar reduction in the calculation time, this approach is interesting in that it uses a connectivity similar to that found in the biological world. This idea is not limited to use in back-propagation models: Fukushima described a model using this idea in the early 1980s [Fuk2], with very interesting results in the area of pattern recognition.

This idea has also been applied successfully to problems of speech recognition, but it seems difficult to generalise the approach to problems other than speech or image processing.

3.4.2   Models which Extend the Network

The learning capacity of a neural network can be significantly enriched if the network is not limited to only modifying synaptic coupling weights as it learns. An alternative form of learning might be to permit the network to grow, by creating additional cells during the process of training with different examples. This model appears completely unacceptable in the biological sense, but the same result can be achieved using a process of differentiation and specialisation of cells rather than straightforward creation.

This mechanism may permit the old-fashioned perceptron idea to win fresh acceptability if it proves possible to find a growth process which compensates for the limits of its synaptic learning ability.

Mezard and Nadal have proposed a family of models of this type, built around very simple basic ideas. They consider the classic classification task: given p boolean vectors of dimension n, separate them into two classes, -1 and $+1$ using a network of threshold neurons.

The growth of the network must follow a set of rules, in order to guarantee the convergence of the algorithm: one neuron on each layer, the first for example, is identified as representing the best current approximation to the desired classification, that is the classification with the least number of wrongly classified examples. The other neurons in each layer C serve solely to preserve information for the final classification. In other words, two input vectors, $X1$ and $X2$, which belong to different classes, must have a different representation at C; the state vectors of this layer when $X1$ and $X2$ are presented, must be different. Each layer is said to give a faithful representation of the examples vis-à-vis the classification.

The convergence requirement demands that the number of classification errors committed by the first unit decreases monatonically from one layer to the next. As the number of training examples is finite, this point guarantees that the algorithm converges when a finite number of layers have been created.

The existence of a solution is simple to demonstrate and is given explicitly in [Mez]. It uses an improved version of the perceptron algorithm, allowing a good solution to be obtained in the case where no linear separation exists. The 'pocket algorithm' operates by preserving the best set of weights, namely the set which gives the smallest number of classification errors, while simultaneously modifying weights using the perceptron rule.

From this general framework, the authors constructed a number of alternative models, the best known of which is the tiling algorithm (see [Mez]). Here we describe a simpler variant (from [Nad1]) in the context of implementing the XOR function.

The network to be used has the following architecture: N boolean input units, M supplementary units, one being the output unit and $M - 1$ being hidden units. Each unit L is connected to all of the input units and to the previous unit $L - 1$.

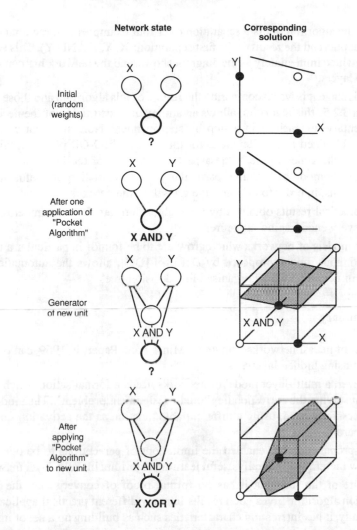

Figure 3.17   An example of growing a network

Whenever the last unit gives an incorrect classification, a further unit is added, one by one.

The representation chosen is the simplest possible with reference to the general model described above, since each hidden layer is presented with the full set of training examples. A proof of the convergence of this algorithm is given in [Nad1], and an example of its use, learning the XOR function, is shown in figure 3.17. The first unit is obtained by applying the perceptron rule on the four cases of the XOR function and ends with an initial linear separation: in this case the AND function.

Next the algorithm finds a separation over four examples in three dimensions (the two inputs and the result of the first separation: X, Y, X AND Y). This separation is obtained immediately as the diagram shows, and the network has converged after two layers.

At this stage it is worth comparing the results of this algorithm and those found in section 3.2.5: this algorithm allows an automatic construction of the necessary supplementary dimensions in a step by step manner. Note also that while the result was obtained in two iterations for the case of the XOR problem, this will be far from the general case. One aspect of the work of the inventors consists of varying the mode of learning, particularly the construction of useful internal representations, in order to optimise the growth of the network.

The practical results obtained by these algorithms are few in number to date, but seem very encouraging in nature.

Other models of networks which grow are to be found: in particular a model with continuous inputs, proposed by Deffuant [Def], allows the automatic construction of neural networks organised like decision trees.

3.5 Summary

The limits of neural networks, shown by Minsky and Papert in 1969, can only be overcome using hidden layers.

However, a multi-layer model of networks needs a formalisation which is capable of resolving the corresponding 'credit assignment problem'. The model has been successfully used, using a differentiable function as the activation function for the neuron.

Back-propagation has enabled the limitations of perceptrons to be overcome and is now therefore a generally useful learning algorithm in multi-layer networks.

In spite of the fact that it has no formal proof of convergence, the back-propagation algorithm gives good results in many different practical applications. Additionally, it has interesting characteristics such as building up a set of internal representations and its capacity for generalisation.

Many questions remain unanswered concerning the back-propagation algorithm, notably those concerning the way in which a network is defined in order to address a particular problem, and the speed of the network's convergence. Active research is underway in an attempt to resolve these questions, and particularly to give a more solid theoretical foundation to back-propagation itself.

Alternative models of multi-layered networks, which allow the network to grow during its learning phase, also seem to be promising.

4 *The Hopfield Model*

This chapter describes undoubtedly the simplest and the best theoretically understood model of neural networks, the fully-connected network. Many extensions of this model and their applications are also described.

4.1 A Content-addressable Memory

Previous parts of the book described the perceptron and back-propagation; although this order of presentation is useful, it does not conform to historical reality.

In 1982, John Hopfield produced a paper entitled 'Neural Networks and Physical Systems with Emergent Collective Computational Abilities' [Ho1]. This paper, clear, well presented and published by a respected physicist, is often considered to have spurred the new interest in neural networks.

The approach of Hopfield is relatively novel, although it calls upon many previous results. According to him, the nervous system attempts to find stable states, attractors, in its state space. Neighbouring states tend to approach a stable state, enabling errors to be corrected and providing the ability to fill in information which is missing.

A Hopfield network is thus a content-addressable memory. A previously memorised shape is looked up by stabilising the network state after stimulating it with a sufficient part of the original shape. Hopfield proposed a model which was capable of implementing these properties, based on a fully interconnected network of the neurons of McCulloch and Pitts [McCu]. The learning rule he used was Hebb's rule [Heb].

One additional contribution of Hopfield to the study of artificial neural networks is the analogy with statistical physics. He showed that during the evolution of the network's state in its approach to stability, an energy function decreases towards a local minimum, in a manner analogous to the behaviour of Ising spin-glasses. This analogy enabled a large number of results from statistical physics to be used in neural networks.

63

4.2   The Model

4.2.1   *A Fully-connected Network*

As described above, the neuron Hopfield uses is that of McCulloch and Pitts. Each neuron has two possible states, $V_i = -1$ and $V_i = 1$. (Hopfield uses 0 and 1 but this is equivalent.) The network consists of N neurons, fully interconnected. The connection from a neuron i to a neuron j is called T_{ij}, as shown in figure 4.1.

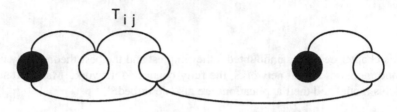

Figure 4.1   Network weights

The sum of the inputs of the neuron i is $I_i = \sum_j T_{ij}Vj$, and the state of the network as a whole is given by the N values V_i, representable by a word of N bits.

The network operates over time, sequenced by a 'clock'. We write:

$V_i(t)$ the state of neuron i at time t

$V_i(t+1)$ the state of neuron i at time $t + \delta t$

The term δt represents the interval between two clock edges.

Each neuron may change its state at a random moment, asynchronously with respect to all others, all neurons changing state with a constant mean frequency. Alternatively, another interpretation is to consider that, at each clock tick, one neuron is selected at random to change state. Each state change is evaluated following the McCulloch and Pitts rule:

$$V_i(t+1) = \begin{cases} +1 \text{ if } \sum_j T_{ij}V_j > 0 \\ -1 \text{ if } \sum_j T_{ij}V_j \leq 0 \end{cases}$$

Alternative rules exist; these are almost equivalent to the original stochastic mode specified by Hopfield. They involve using a synchronous updating method, in which all of the neurons change state simultaneously, or a sequential method in which the neurons change one after another in a defined order.

The neuron model chosen is the same as that of the perceptron, but the resemblance stops there. The Hopfield model is recursive, with bidirectional connections, while connections are unidirectional in the layered models; secondly the perceptron model, requiring synchronisation between all of its neurons, is less biologically plausible.

4.2.2 Learning in Hopfield Networks

Learning in Hopfield networks is sometimes described as rote learning, to distinguish it from learning methods based on trial and error. In fact the connection weights can be directly calculated, given the full set of states to be memorised. The problem is as follows: suppose that a Hopfield network is desired to memorise a set of states V^s, where $s = 1 \ldots n$. These states are called *prototypes*.

Used in this context, 'memorising' means that all of the V states must be stable states of the network, following the state dynamics described above. In addition, there must be attractor states, which enable each stable state to be reached from states that are slightly different.

In order to produce this effect, Hopfield used connection weights as follows:

$$T_{ij} = \sum_s V_i^s V_j^s$$
$$T_{ii} = 0$$

It may be simply demonstrated that these weights can be found using a quantitative application of the Hebb rule [Heb]. The Hebb rule consists of increasing the weight of a connection between two neurons every time that the two neurons are simultaneously active. In a Hopfield network, this can be expressed in the following manner: the network starts with a completely null set of connections (the null hypothesis), and the network is forced into a particular state V^s. Each of the possible pairs of neurons (i, j) are examined and the weight T_{ij} is increased by ΔT_{ij}, where ΔT_{ij} is calculated according to the following table:

V_i^s	V_j^s	ΔT_{ij}	
+1	+1	+1	neurons simultaneously active
+1	−1	−1	neurons in opposition
−1	+1	−1	neurons in opposition
−1	−1	+1	neurons simultaneously inactive

It will be seen that as each training example is presented successively, the value of the weights throughout the network will become higher or lower.

Other different formulations of the Hebb rule are sometimes found, some conforming better to a biological intuition than others; in some cases, if two neurons are simultaneously inactive, it would seem better to leave the weight of the connection between them unchanged rather than increasing it as in the table above.

The alteration value, ΔT, may be expressed simply as a linear combination of symmetric functions of V_i^s and V_j^s.

Generally, the weight of the connection (i, j) is a measure of the correlation between the firing of neurons i and j over the full set of examples which have been taught.

4.2.3 Stability of States

Following from the definition of T_{ij}, we have

$$\sum_j T_{ij} V_j^s = \sum_j \left(\sum_t V_i^t V_j^t \right) V_j^s$$

$$= \sum_t V_i^t \left(\sum_j V_j^t V_j^s \right)$$

$$= \sum_t V_i^t \langle V^s V^t \rangle$$

Note that a sufficient condition for stability is that the states are orthogonal one with another, in which case we have

$$\sum_j T_{ij} V_j^s = V_i^s(t)$$

This condition is not necessary, since a sufficient condition to ensure stability is when $\sum_j T_{ij} V_j^s$ and $V_i^s(t)$ have the same sign.

Thus we see that the Hebb rule at least ensures the stability of states which are orthogonal.

An important notion in the Hopfield networks is that of a basin of attraction. If V^s is a stable state, we note that

$$B(V^s) = \{V, \text{ such that } T^n V = V^s\}$$

In this expression, T is the transformation of summation and thresholding, which forms the basis of the dynamics of states.

The basin of attraction of a state V^s is thus the set of states V of the network which evolve towards V^s after a finite number of transitions. In order to obtain maximum noise immunity, it is necessary to widen this basin as far as possible around states that are used to memorise information.

4.2.4 Conclusions

The Hopfield model is quite different to the multi-layered models introduced earlier; its learning process is basically static, since there is no true dynamics of connections, but rather the operation of the network (or its relaxation) is dynamic. The network may take a number of iterations before reaching a stable state.

We note that learning, as defined in Hopfield networks, is incremental: in order to add a new stable state to the network, it is only necessary to modify the weights T_{ij} using the Hebb rule.

Hopfield networks are often described as enabling the implementation of self-associative memories: an input such as a shape or a word, incomplete or partly obscured by noise, is forced into the network. The dynamics of the network allow it to converge towards a stable state which is, in general, the state that is desired.

There is no significant difference between auto-associative memory and hetero-associative memory. We have shown earlier that it is possible to use back-propagation as self-associative memory, for image compression, for example. In the same way, Hopfield networks can be used as hetero-associative memories: states which were in pairs, for example a name and a telephone number, could be memorised. Once these states were memorised, if the name alone was input to the network, the state dynamics would, in principle, find the complete couple and thus find the telephone number.

Limits and Difficulties

The definition of weights by the Hebb rule in Hopfield networks may introduce stable states which are not *a priori* desired. These 'rubbish states' may ultimately form strong attractors. Different solutions have been suggested to overcome this problem. One solution [Pop] is based on the principle of trial and error: the weights are modified in order to widen the basin of attraction of desired states and to diminish that of rubbish states. This is done by setting the network into a neighbour state of a stable state, and allowing it to stabilise. If the network stabilises into a rubbish state or into a state different from that desired, the connection weights are modified as a consequence. This process is repeated until all the states neighbouring desired stable states converge in the desired manner.

Hopfield proposes a model of 'unlearning' in [Ho3]. The network is randomly initialised and when it converges, the state into which it stabilises is slightly 'unlearned' in the sense that the Hebb rule is applied in the reverse direction with a small coefficient. If the network stabilises itself in state V^s, the connections are modified in the manner

$$\Delta T_{ij} = -\mu V_i^s V_j^s, \text{with } \mu \ll 1$$

According to Hopfield, this process allows the attractiveness of rubbish states to be decreased, whilst increasing that of desired states.

Another problem is that of the orthogonality of stable states. This is not a necessary condition but the prototypes must satisfy a very restrictive condition of pseudo-orthogonality, which may not have any relevance to a real problem. How, for example, is it possible to ensure that telephone numbers are 'orthogonal'? Personnaz, Dreyfus and Guyon [Per], used the 'projection rule' to calculate weights. The matrix of connection weights is the matrix of orthogonal projection on the vector subspace given by the prototypes to be learned. Their method ensures the stability of these prototypes regardless of whether or not they are orthogonal. This method is similar to the adaptive filter method of Kohonen, described in chapter 5.

The Hopfield model has been studied very intensively, largely due to its analogy with physical systems. In particular, results have been obtained on the storage capacity of such a network: theoretical results from physics research, and numerous simulations show that the optimum ratio between the number of examples to be learned and the number of neurons is in the region of 0.14. However, if further examples are learned, the Hopfield network shows a very undesirable characteristic: it forgets catastrophically. A network may learn N examples without difficulty and forget them all when it is taught one additional example.

This problem has been studied in detail and a model of learning which enables progressive forgetting to take place has been proposed in [Nad].

4.3   Use in Optimisation Problems

4.3.1   Energy in Hopfield Networks

Consider a Hopfield network with N cells with the customary notation. Following Hopfield, the energy function H, characterising the state of the network, is introduced:

$$H(V) = -\frac{1}{2}\sum_i \sum_j T_{ij}V_iV_j \qquad (1)$$

Note that the variation of H for a variation ΔV_i in the state V_i of the neuron i, is given by

$$\begin{aligned}\Delta H &= -\tfrac{1}{2}\Delta V_i \sum_j T_{ij}V_j \\ &= -\tfrac{1}{2}\Delta V_i I_i \end{aligned} \qquad (2)$$

Consider the variation in V_i undergone by a neuron following the rule of operation for the network:

$$\Delta V_i = V_i(t+1) - V_i(t)$$

The following table is obtained, showing the value of ΔV_i as a function of $V_i(t)$ and $I_i(t)$, the total input of the neuron at time t.

$V_i(t)$	$I_i(t)$	ΔV_i	ΔH
+1	> 0	0	0
+1	< 0	−2	< 0
−1	> 0	+2	< 0
−1	< 0	0	0

Consider for example, the second line in the table. If the neuron is in state 1 at time t and its total input is negative, then following the operating rule, it moves to state −1. ΔV_i is therefore −2 and, following equation 2, the total energy variation in the system is negative. The table therefore shows that the energy function H

always decreases when the network follows the operating rule defined by Hopfield. All the stable states of the network are local minima of the energy function H.

Hopfield's introduction of this energy function, which was derived from the model of Ising spin-glasses, enabled a large number of results from statistical physics to be applied and motivated physicists to study Hopfield neural networks. For example, Nadal, Toulouse, Dehane and Changeux used results from the theory of spin-glasses in [Nad2] to give an explanation of catastrophic forgetting and to quantify the number of prototypes that a network of N neurons is capable of memorising.

4.3.2 A Dual Problem

Energy defined here is in a quadratic form. It is defined for a network with fixed connection weights, and we have stated that the operation of this network, following the Hopfield rule, leads to local minima of this energy function.

A dual formulation of this problem is therefore possible; it was introduced by Hopfield himself in [Ho4].

We consider a system parameterised by N state variables, $E_1, E_2, \ldots, E_n$, each of which may take the value -1 or $+1$. E, the state of the system, is the n-tuple $(E_1, E_2, \ldots, E_n)$. If one imagines that a cost function $H(E)$ is defined for this system, and further that H is a symmetric quadratic function of E_i, the problem of minimising H can be resolved by a Hopfield network.

It is sufficient to construct a network whose connection weights are the coefficients of the quadratic equation for H.

The value of this method is the result that optimisation problems may therefore be solved by simulating the corresponding Hopfield network, using a parallel algorithm.

There are two possible objections to this suggestion: the class of problems which may be addressed in this manner seems to be limited to those with quadratic form and secondly, the minimisation obtained is only local, and not global.

We show below that difficult problems in optimisation, NP complete problems, in all cases, may be addressed in this manner; in addition, we show how the problem of local minima may find a solution within a similar framework.

4.3.3 The Travelling Salesman Problem

The travelling salesman problem is very simply expressed: a small solution is shown in figure 4.2. It involves finding the shortest path connecting N towns, passing through each town once, and once only. The number of possible paths is $N!/2N$ which is more than 10^{30} for 30 towns. There are many partial solutions which do not involve exhaustive search, but the use of parallel algorithms is the best solution if N becomes large.

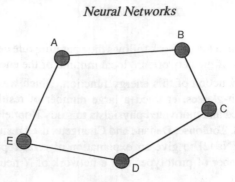

Figure 4.2   The travelling salesman problem

step	1	2	3	4	5
A	0	1	0	0	0
B	0	0	0	1	0
towns C	1	0	0	0	0
D	0	0	1	0	0
E	0	0	0	0	1

Figure 4.3   The solution table

One method of solving this problem was proposed by Hopfield in [Ho4].

It consists of defining a system characterised by a binary set of state variables and a quadratic energy function over this system, such that the solutions to the problem, the shortest paths, are minima of this energy function by construction.

Hopfield chose to characterise this system using a table of towns and steps: an entry (X, i) is 1 if town X is visited at step i, and 0 otherwise. One possible table is shown in figure 4.3. Values of 0 and 1 are used rather than -1 and $+1$ in order to simplify calculation.

This set of variables allows a particular path to be completely specified. At the same time, many possible states of the system are illegal: a legal state has exactly one 1 in each row and each column, meaning that each town is visited once and once only, and that only one town may be visited at each step.

These states are represented on a network of N^2 neurons, each neuron representing one table entry.

The problem thus becomes that of selecting the connections between neurons so that illegal states are very disfavoured, in energy terms, and so that the lowest energy states correspond to the shortest paths.

Energy is defined to achieve these goals, using a sum of a number of terms.

We use V_{Xi} to represent the variable at the intersection of row X and column i. V_{Xi} is 1 or 0, depending on whether town X is visited at step i.

The first energy term, C_1, acts to disfavour states in which there are two or more 1's in a single row X.

$$C_1 = \sum_X \sum_i \sum_{j \neq i} V_{Xi} V_{Xj}$$

In the same way a term C_2 serves to make the states where there are two 1's in a column i less popular

$$C_2 = \sum_i \sum_X \sum_{Y \neq X} V_{Xi} V_{Yi}$$

Finally, a term C_3 forces the system to stabilise in states where there are exactly N entries in the table set to 1

$$C_3 = (\sum_X \sum_i V_{Xi} - N)^2$$

These three terms are called constraint terms. They allow the system to be prohibited from entering illegal states. The last term is the only one in which the criterion to be minimised, the length of the path, actually appears

$$M = \sum_X \sum_{Y \neq X} \sum_i d_{XY} V_{Xi} (V_{Y,i+1} + V_{Y,i-1})$$

(In this final term, d_{XY} represents the distance between X and Y and the indices are expressed in modulo N.) The total energy of the system is thus given by

$$H = -aC_1 - bC_2 - cC_3 - dM$$

After calculation, the weights of the coefficients between neurons are deduced using the Cronecker notation ($\delta_{ij} = 1$ if, and only if $i = j$)

$$T_{Xi,Yj} = -a\delta_{XY}(1 - \delta_{ij}) - bd_{ij}(1 - \delta_{XY}) - c \quad dd_{XY}(\delta_{j,i+1} + \delta_{j,i-1})$$

In [Ho4], Hopfield gives useful values for the coefficients a, b, c and d and shows that this problem, implemented on neural networks, converges to 'good' solutions in a high proportion of cases.

However, some comments are in order. Hopfield uses a formulation of the problem where legality constraints and the function to be minimised are mixed up together. Whilst this solution is simple, it is far from being efficient in that much time is lost in avoiding states which are simply illegal.

The problem of local minima is not overcome: in particular, in order to guarantee that the network converges to good solutions, the derivation of the parameters a, b, c and d is not straightforward.

4.4 Simulated Annealing

4.4.1 A Thermodynamic Analogy

The simulated annealing algorithm was introduced in 1983 by Kirkpatrick, Gelatt and Vecchi [Kir]. It is based on the work of Metropolis dating from the 1950s [Met].

The method uses an analogy with thermodynamics. If we consider a system consisting of a large number of particles and we characterise a state of this system as the data giving the state of all of these particles, for example, the position or the magnetic moment of each atom, then the probability of finding this system in a given state is proportional to the Boltzmann factor $\exp(-H(E)/T)$ where H represents the energy of this state. Thus the probability of two states, E_1 and E_2 occurring are related by the relationship:

$$\frac{p(e1)}{p(e2)} = \exp\left[\frac{-(H(e1) - H(e2))}{T}\right]$$

Metropolis proposed a simple algorithm to simulate such a set of atoms in equilibrium at a given temperature T. At each step in the simulation one atom is given a random displacement and the variation in energy, ΔH, of the system, is calculated. If $\Delta H \leq 0$, the displacement is carried out. The case where $\Delta H > 0$ is processed in a probabilistic manner. The probability of accepting the displacement is $p = \exp(-\Delta H/T)$.

In the simulated annealing algorithm, the energy is replaced by a cost function which needs minimising and the method of Metropolis is used to explore the states of the system. Temperature is an input parameter which, when high, enables large energy changes to take place. The idea of simulated annealing is to set this temperature to a high value at the beginning of the simulation so that the system explores a large number of states. When the system seems to have stabilised, the temperature is gradually lowered and the procedure is repeated until $T = 0$.

This principle is inspired by the annealing process in metallurgy: the temperature of a crystal is raised and then very slowly lowered in order to obtain a very pure and very well-formed crystal.

This method of minimising a real function can be explained intuitively by considering the graph of figure 4.4. An initial state x_0 is used at the beginning of the simulation. T is set to a high value at the beginning. At each stage the possibility of varying x by Δx in an arbitrary direction is considered. The variation is accepted or not following the Metropolis rule. When T is high, significant steps on the graph are accepted, which should lead x with a high probability to the neighbourhood of a global minimum. The temperature T is successively decreased progressively in order to 'freeze' the variable. A method using gradient descent would have a high probability of reaching just a local minimum in this problem.

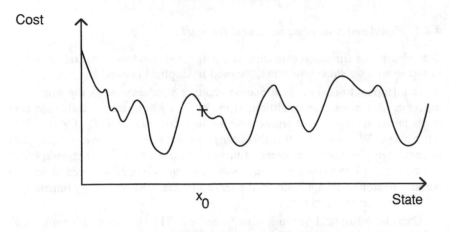

Figure 4.4   How to find the lowest energy?

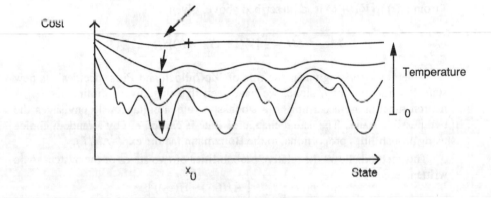

Figure 4.5   Finding low energy states as T falls

Another intuitive representation of this algorithm is to imagine a ball free to move on an energy surface corresponding to H. Initially, the surface is agitated a great deal (T is high), in order that the ball can pass from one valley to another, then progressively the agitation is diminished (T decreases) in order to trap the ball in one of the deepest valleys. Finally, the agitation is completely stopped so that the ball falls to the very bottom of this valley, which corresponds to an absolute minimum of the function H.

Alternatively, the temperatures can be seen as a way of smoothing out the shape of the energy function, as shown in figure 4.5. At the beginning, high temperatures level out the function. Progressive lowering of the temperature allows all of the hilliness to be explored gently.

4.4.2   Simulated Annealing in Neural Networks

The principle of simulated annealing is *a priori* independent of neural networks. In this section we show how it may be used in Hopfield networks.

In a Hopfield network, each neuron changes state as soon as the sum of its inputs satisfies some sign condition. If the neuron was in state 1 and if the sum of its inputs is negative, it enters state −1 and operates similarly for the three other cases. We have seen that this change of state always moves in the sense of decreasing the associated energy function. In order to have a network which functions according to the principle of simulated annealing all we need to do is to permit a neuron to change states in the sense of increasing the energy function, as a function of some temperature.

Consider a Hopfield network with n neurons. The state of each neuron is V_i and the total state of the system is thus characterised by $V = (V_1, V_2, \ldots, V_n)$. Following Hopfield's state dynamics, neurons change states as a function of their total input. The variation of energy corresponding to a change in state of neuron i from $V_i(t)$ to $V_i(t+1)$ is, as described above, given by

$$\Delta H = \frac{1}{2}\,[V_i(t+1) - V_i(t)]\,I_i$$

A neuron operating under the rule of McCulloch and Pitts 'decides' its new state as a function of I_i alone; we have seen that this always diminishes H. A neuron functioning according to a stochastic rule simultaneously envisages the two possible states. The actual change of state is carried out by a random choice using probabilities proportional to the Boltzmann factor: $\exp(-\Delta H/T)$.

This method allows the relative probabilities of two states of the system to be written:

$$\frac{p(e_1)}{p(e_2)} = \exp\left[\frac{-(H(e_1) - H(e_2))}{T}\right]$$

The Boltzmann factors relating the four possible different pairings of V_i and $V_i(t+1)$ are shown in figure 4.6. When probabilities are normalised, they give the values shown below:

$$p(V_{i(t+1)} = +1) = 1/[1 + \exp(-I_i/T)]$$
$$p(V_{i(t+1)} = -1) = \exp(-I_i/T)/[1 + \exp(-I_i/T)]$$

		$V_i(t+1)$	
		+1	+1
V_i	+1	1	$\exp(-I_i/T)$
	−1	$\exp(I_i/T)$	1

Figure 4.6   Boltzmann factors relating two states

Finally, we see that the new state of the stochastic neuron is independent of its previous state.

We can also state that as T tends towards 0, the stochastic neuron tends towards the threshold neuron of McCulloch and Pitts.

It is thus possible to apply the principle of simulated annealing to the operation of a neural network minimising quadratic functions, and solving problems such as the travelling salesman problem. All that is required is to use a fully interconnected Hopfield neural network, to use neurons with a functioning rule which is stochastic, to choose an annealing sequence, that is a decreasing set of temperatures and to select, for each temperature, the number of transitions to carry out.

Example

We give here another example of the formulation of a problem in the form of minimisation of a quadratic function. This example is taken from [Kir].

The problem of partitioning frequently occurs when integrated circuits are designed. There are N elements which need to be allocated between two chips so that the number of connections between the two chips is reduced as far as possible. The number of connections between two elements i and j is imposed by the design of the circuit and is symbolised a_{ij}.

The other constraint is that it is frequently desired to partition the two chips as equally as possible. If this were not so, the ideal solution would be to place all of the elements on one chip!

The variable μ_i takes the value 1, if element i is on chip 1 and -1 if it is on chip 2. We calculate N_c, the number of connections between the two chips. Therefore,

$$N_c = \sum_{i>j} a_{ij}[(\mu_i - \mu_j)/2]^2$$

In other words, $\sum_i \mu_i$ represents the difference between the number of elements on the chip 1 and the number of elements on the chip 2. To resolve the problem we simply need to minimise

$$H = \sum_{i>j} a_{ij}[(\mu_i - \mu_j)/2]^2 + \beta \left(\sum_i \mu_i\right)^2$$

which is written

$$H = H_0 + \sum_{i>j} (\beta - a_{ij}/2)\mu_i\mu_j$$

H is a symmetric, quadratic form in μ_i and can thus be minimised on a neural network, using simulated annealing.

Many other examples of problems which may be specified in these terms are contained in [Kir].

4.5   The Boltzmann Machine

4.5.1   Description

The principle of simulated annealing improves the *state dynamics* of a Hopfield network, enabling local minima to be avoided. Simulated annealing therefore allows us to improve the 'dual' use of Hopfield networks described above: finding the state which gives the minimum energy of the network. For this application, it is necessary to design a *connection dynamics* for the initial use of such a network; a learning algorithm which allows minima to be created where desired, that is, in locations determined by the data to be memorised.

In 1985, Ackley, Hinton and Sejnowski, in [Ack], proposed a learning algorithm for a network using simulated annealing: the Boltzmann machine.

This algorithm is very different from those described to date. In this section, it is introduced intuitively, and a more formal description follows.

Prototypes and Stable States

Consider a set P of p vectors of N components, each component taking the value 0 or 1. These vectors need to be memorised in a Hopfield-type network, and are commonly called prototype or example vectors. An arbitrary vector space with N dimensions has 2^N possible vectors, and the data given by P can be seen as on particular probability distribution within this space. This probability distribution might take the form of assigning a probability $1/p$ for a vector belonging to P and a probability 0 for every other vector.

Separately, consider a Hopfield network with N stochastic neurons operating using a simulated annealing process. If this network is preset to an arbitrary initial state, and allowed to operate, it will reach a particular stable state. (If the temperature is non-zero it will reach a stationary probability distribution of states: the thermal equilibrium.) If this process is repeated a large number of times, noting the stable state reached each time, the probabilities of reaching each of the possible 2^N network states can be measured.

The idea underlying the learning process in a Boltzmann machine is to construct a network such that probabilities defined by the set of its stable states is equal to the set of probabilities defined by the prototype data.

Energy in the Stable States and Connection Weights

Considering a Hopfield network with N stochastic neurons, using simulated annealing, the probability that this network is in a particular state, at a given temperature T, depends upon the energy of that state and upon T, as described in section 4.4. Thus the probability of a global state of the network can be modified by changing that state's energy.

The energy of such a network, following Hopfield's definition, is strongly dependent on the weights of the connections between the neurons. The remaining problem in learning is to impose a certain set of probabilities for the global states of the network by varying the weights on individual connections between neurons.

Connection Weights and Correlations

The question arises: is it possible to impose an arbitrary set of probabilities on the global states of the network simply by varying the weights of connections between neurons? A simple example shows that this is insufficient, since varying the weight of a single connection between two neurons simply alters the correlation of activity between these two neurons, that is the probability that these two neurons are simultaneously active. Consider, for example, a network of three neurons in which the distribution of probabilities corresponding to the XOR function given below is to be learned.

$$p = 1/4 \quad \text{for } (110), (101), (011) \text{ and } (000)$$
$$p = 0 \quad \text{for the other four triples}$$

At the same time, consider the distribution of probabilities which corresponds to the full set of possible states

$$p = 1/8 \text{ for each of 8 triples}$$

If the correlations between all possible pairs of neurons is calculated for each of these two state distributions, they are found to be the same. Therefore, the two probability distributions are indistinguishable using solely the correlations between each possible pair of neurons. These two distributions can only be distinguished when considering correlations with an order higher than 2.

The fundamental new idea for learning in a Boltzmann machine consisted of adding units in excess of the N necessary to the network. This enlarged network is still treated in the same way and is altered only by changing the weights on connections between neurons, but higher order correlations over N neurons may be represented by correlations of order 2 on a larger network.

Forced and Free Modes

Consider a network of $N + m$ neurons. We call the N fundamental units of this network *visible units*, corresponding to the dimension of our set of examples; the m other neurons are called *hidden units*.

The learning process will still attempt to impose a probability distribution on this network, but it seems that the introduction of hidden units means that the correct distribution is no longer obvious. The set of prototypes has dimension N and gives no indication of the desired state of the m hidden units.

A *forced* mode of operation in the network is therefore introduced, permitting the probability distribution over the $N + m$ units to be estimated. Consider a data prototype of dimension N. If the state of the visible units of the network is constrained to the values of this prototype and the hidden units are permitted to operate normally, the entire network can reach a certain stable state. If this process is repeated for all prototypes, a large number of times, a distribution of probabilities over the full set of $N + m$ units in the network can be estimated.

Considering also the *free* mode of operation of the network, the original mode of operation in which no unit is fixed, a new formulation of the learning process in a Boltzmann machine is reached. Learning consists of making the probability distribution of global states of the network in the free mode the same as the distribution in forced mode.

4.5.2 Formal Description

Hopfield Networks

Consider a network of $N + m$ stochastic neurons, divided into a set of visible units and a set of hidden units. V_i is the state (0 or 1) of the neuron i, and T_{ij} is the weight of the connection between neuron i and neuron j. Suppose this system is at a temperature T at a particular instance. Consider the two modes of operation of the Boltzmann machine, the free mode in which the values of certain units are fixed at the start, each neuron subsequently evolving according to its stochastic rule, and the forced mode in which the value of certain units is held constant, all other neurons operating freely.

In the free mode each neuron evaluates its new state according to the rules given in section 4.2

$$p(V_{i(t+1)=1}) = 1/[1 + \exp(-I_i/T)]$$
$$p(V_{i(t+1)=0}) = \exp(-I_i/T)/[1 + \exp(-I_i/T)]$$

In the forced mode, only the hidden units operate in this manner.

Distance Between Probability Distributions

Given a global state of the network A, we define

$P(A)$ the probability of A occurring in the free mode
$Q(A)$ the probability of A occurring in the forced mode

Following the learning principle of Boltzmann machines, the distance between the probability distribution of the states in free mode and that in forced mode is to be minimised. A measure of this distance from information theory is used:

$$G = \sum_A Q(A) \log[Q(A)/P(A)]$$

It is demonstrated in [Ack] that

$$\frac{\delta G}{\delta T_{ij}} = -\frac{1}{T}(p^+{}_{ij} - p^-{}_{ij})$$

Note that $p^+{}_{ij}$ and $p^-{}_{ij}$ represent the probability that units i and j are simultaneously active in the forced mode or in the free mode respectively.

The process of learning thus consists of minimising the function G using gradient descent.

The Learning Algorithm

As described above, if the probabilities $p^+{}_{ij}$ and $p^-{}_{ij}$ are directly measurable from the example data, and i and j are both visible units, these probabilities must be estimated for the hidden units. The learning algorithm is given below.

Forced Phase

An example is imposed on the visible units, and the network is permitted to relax to thermal equilibrium, using an annealing sequence. Finally, the pairs of the network neurons that are simultaneously active are noted. This process is repeated for different examples, permitting $p^+{}_{ij}$ to be estimated.

Free Phase

The same operations are carried out, without imposing any value on any unit, and $p^-{}_{ij}$ is estimated.

Once these two phases have been carried out, each weight may be modified using a term proportional to

$$\Delta T_{ij} = \mu\frac{1}{T}(p^+{}_{ij} - p^+{}_{ij})$$

These steps are repeated and repeated, until a minimum of G is reached.

Association in a Boltzmann Machine

One variant of this learning algorithm allows a Boltzmann machine to act as an associative device. The set of visible units is divided into input units and output units. In the forced mode the input units and the output units are both maintained constant. In the free mode only the input units are kept constant. Similar results to those outlined above can be obtained.

4.5.3   Conclusion

The learning algorithm in Boltzmann machines was the first model to propose solutions using hidden units in a neural network, introducing the notion of internal representation of features of the problem.

However, the calculation power necessary to implement a Boltzmann machine is very large; one single step in the learning process necessitates the estimation of a probability distribution. This algorithm has been little used in real applications to date.

4.6   Summary

The Hopfield model allows the study of fully-connected neural networks, using the Hebb rule to change connection weights, and operating stochastically. Formally this model is very simple, giving rise to interesting results in self-association and hetero-association. Nevertheless, in its simplest version, it presents a number of problems such as rubbish states and catastrophic forgetting.

A physical analogy, obtained by introducing an energy function, allows this model to be studied using results from statistical physics; theoretical results include a relationship between the size of a network and its capacity to memorise a given number of facts.

The 'thermodynamic' point of view allows a dual use of Hopfield networks in optimisation problems. A Hopfield network may be used to automatically minimise a quadratic equation. This use of the network is improved using a simulated annealing process, again derived from thermodynamics, which provides a partial solution to the problem of local minima.

Finally, the statistical approach may be used to construct a learning algorithm, based on simulated annealing, in a neural network called the Boltzmann machine. This algorithm gives a solution to the 'credit assignment problem' in a network which uses hidden units.

5 *The Kohonen Model*

The models described in chapters 3 and 4 may be better known, but the work of another researcher, Teuvo Kohonen, characterised by its richness and formal rigour, is also worth studying. This chapter describes the broad outlines of his work and introduces the general framework of his neural network studies. Finally, different models that he has proposed are covered, with descriptions of their neurobiological foundation, their mathematical development and their applications.

5.1 A General Model

5.1.1 The Synthetic Neuron

Kohonen's synthetic neuron is very close to the models described previously. It is characterised by a state variable which is both its activation level and its output. This variable, S, takes only positive values.

Kohonen uses a dynamic equation of state:

$$\frac{dS}{dt} = E - p(S)$$

E is the total input (see later) and $p(S)$ is a non-linear loss term which allows the phenomenon of saturation to be taken into account, thus limiting the frequency with which a neuron can fire. This implies a limitation on the speed of changing of the neuron states.

Kohonen studied the case following the stabilisation of the neuron, that is from the time when the neuron, after receiving a number of inputs, has completed its intermediate rapid changes in state and gives an output that is stable over a long time interval. In other words the neuron changes from one state to another by making a series of rapid transitions which are of no interest to us. This stable state is characterised by the equation:

$$\frac{dS}{dt} = 0$$

81

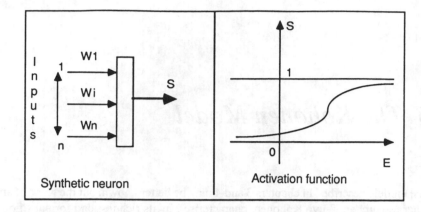

Figure 5.1   Kohonen's neuron model

The solution of this gives the law of operation of the neuron

$$S = p^{-1}(E) = p^{-1}\left(\sum_{i=1,n} W_i E_i\right)$$

The function p^{-1} is a sigmoid function. In this way the classic schema, shown in figure 5.1, is obtained. In the figure, E is given by

$$E = \sum_{i=1,n} W_i E_i$$

5.1.2   The Learning Mechanism

The learning mechanism is based on the fact that the Hebb rule, when neuron activation can take only positive values, cannot reduce the value of the weight of connections when one of two neurons is inactive. This implies that the learning mechanism cannot contribute to the phenomenon of forgetting as a result of either activity or inactivity of neurons.

Kohonen proposed the following equation as a learning rule:

$$\frac{dW_i}{dt} = kSe_i - \beta(S)W_i$$

In this equation, $\beta(S) > 0$ is a function to implement forgetting and $k \geq 0$ normally.

The learning mechanism operates as follows: if the neuron receives an action potential via its connection i and if it is active, this connection is reinforced. If the

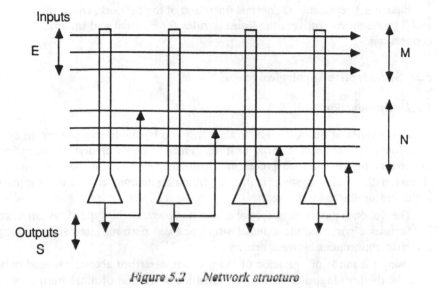

Inputs

E

M

N

Outputs
S

Figure 5.2   Network structure

neuron receives no action potential via connection i or if, following the receipt of a potential via this connection, it does not activate, the weight of this connection is diminished.

5.1.3   The Structure of the Network

Kohonen proposed a very simple structure which could be refined according to the needs of different applications. The architecture, shown in figure 5.2, simultaneously takes account of external data arriving at the network and of internal connections of the network.

$S = (S_1, \ldots, S_i, \ldots, S_n)$ is the output vector of the n neurons in the network;

$E = (E_1, \ldots, E_i, \ldots, E_m)$ is the input vector from the m external inputs to the network;

M is the matrix of weights on the connections from external inputs to the neurons;

N is the matrix of weights on the connections between neurons in the network.

The Kohonen model is characterised by three dynamic state equations describing the operation of the network and its learning.

$$\frac{\mathrm{d}S}{\mathrm{d}t} = F(E, S, M, N) \quad (1)$$

$$\frac{\mathrm{d}M}{\mathrm{d}t} = G(E, S, M) \quad (2)$$

$$\frac{\mathrm{d}N}{\mathrm{d}t} = H(S, N) \quad (3)$$

Equation 1 represents the normal operation of the network, while equations 2 and 3 represent respectively the learning rules for external and internal network connections.

5.2   Self-adaptive Topological Maps

5.2.1   Introduction

These are types of networks which were inspired by modelling perception systems found in mammals, such as hearing. These systems involve the reception of external signals and their processing inside the nervous system. The primary characteristic of these systems is that neighbouring neurons encode input signals which are similar to each other.

The Kohonen model, described above, can implement this type of system since it possesses a port onto the external world and can perform internal processing using the connections between neurons.

Using the mode of operation of the neurons described above, we need only describe the learning rules. Kohonen based his derivation of these starting with biological observations concerning the mechanisms of interactions between neurons and the fact that certain neurons play very specific roles. The consequences of these observations are described below and examples of operation and of applications are then described.

5.2.2   Specialised Neurons

Electrical methods, newly developed for investigating neurobiology, have shown certain nerve cells to have very specific tasks in perception systems: for example, in a study of the visual system of cats, it was shown that certain neurons react specifically to the presence of an inclined feature in one particular part of the field of vision [Mes].

Kohonen developed the idea of creating a network in which each of its neurons react in a specific manner to one single type of stimulus. He calls this type of network 'a network with localised responses'. In figure 5.3, S_i is the localised response to the signal E. S_i is the most active output of the network.

This localised response corresponds to a particular characteristic of the signal at the input. If we imagine using this network to solve a problem of classification, each specific output neuron is associated with each class of inputs. For example, in character recognition, each output neuron would correspond to one character of the alphabet.

5.2.3   Lateral Interaction Between Neurons

Other studies of biology have shown that there is a lateral interaction mechanism which depends on the distance between neurons receiving signals from receptor

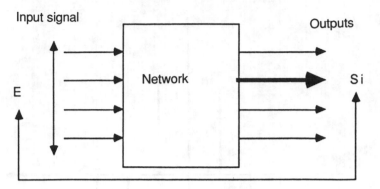

Figure 5.3   The response to E is localised

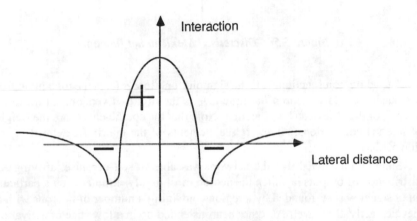

Figure 5.4   Mexican hat function

cells [Koh]. This dependence is represented by a function, shown in figure 5.4, called 'the Mexican hat', whose curve is interpreted as follows: in a lateral zone close to one particular neuron, the neurons connected to it have an excitor function; in an area further away, their action is inhibitory; the action of the furthest neurons is negligible.

In order to understand the influences of these lateral interactions, Kohonen simulated a one-dimensional network (simplifying the problem of determining the lateral zones of excitation and inhibition), applying an input signal and then allowing the network to settle down. Using the notation defined above, the neuron rule of operation is:

$$S_i(t) = f\left[E_i(t) + \sum_{k=-m,+m} I_k S_{i+k}(t-1)\right]$$

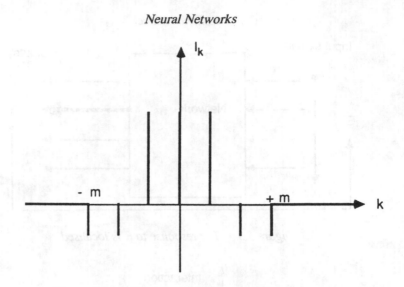

Figure 5.5   Discretised Mexican hat function

The activation function, f, is the sigmoid function; $E_i(t)$ is the total input from the outside world to neuron i at time t; I_k is the digitised version, shown in figure 5.5, of the 'Mexican hat' function. Note that the coefficients I_k are the weights of internal connections: these are the elements in the matrix N, defined in section 5.1.3.

Simulation showed that the network was able to self-organise, arriving at a distribution of outputs in which the neuron most highly stimulated by a particular input signal was surrounded by a region containing a number of neurons with an elevated activation level. All other neurons ended up in a low state of activation.

5.2.4   Consequences

In order to simulate networks following the two neurobiological observations described above, two points must be observed: each cell of the network must respond to one specific input stimulus, and lateral interaction between neurons must cause the group of neurons around the neuron most highly activated by the stimulus to be partially excited. To reach these goals in such a network, only the weights of external connections are modified during the learning process. The weights of internal connections are fixed, defined by the discrete version of the 'Mexican hat' function.

The learning rule proposed by Kohonen is specified in two stages, allowing the two important points to be addressed separately. First the neuron corresponding to the given input signal is selected and secondly, the activation of this neuron, and of the group of neurons surrounding, is increased when this input signal is presented. This serves to increase the correlation between this neuron and its neighbours for the particular input signal under consideration.

This type of network is called a 'map' by Kohonen because it preserves any topological relations found in the input signal on its map of neuron activations. In other words if two input shapes are similar, they will be represented by two output neurons or groups of neurons which share the same neighbourhood. This is the case in the auditory system: the neuronal map showing which cells in the cortex are sensitive to each particular frequency is close to a simple logarithmic function of frequency.

5.2.5 A Simple Two-dimensional Autonomous System

This network is used to illustrate the points described in previous chapters and to demonstrate the learning rule used by Kohonen. Consider the general network of section 5.1.3, shown in figure 5.6. From this network, a two-dimensional network is developed by arranging neurons in an array, shown in figure 5.7: each neuron is connected to all of the input signals. The interactions between neurons are determined by the lateral interaction defined by the 'Mexican hat' function: the internal connection matrix is fully specified.

The two principles of the learning rule defined in section 5.2.4 are now applied. The learning rule may only vary the weights of external connections.

The first step is to select one neuron to correspond to a particular input signal. Remember that the vector of external connection weights for a neuron i which receives input vectors of dimension m, is written $(M_{ij})_{i \leq j \leq m}$.

Kohonen proposed an interesting means of associating particular neurons with different input classes: he suggested that a particular input vector can be regarded as the image of neuron i in the vector space defined by the set of input signals

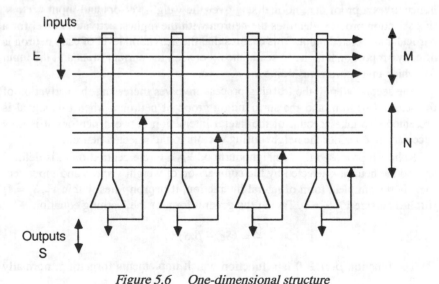

Figure 5.6   One-dimensional structure

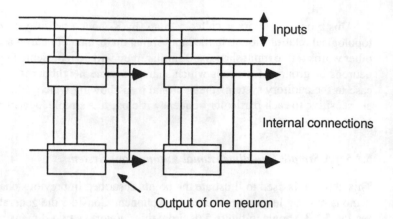

Figure 5.7　Two-dimensional structure

[Koh]. He proposed that the choice be made by comparing each neuron's vector of connection weights with the current input vector, choosing the neuron whose weights most closely approximate the vector. This technique distinguishes Kohonen's auto-adaptive map topologies from all networks previously described.

Thus, when a signal E is presented, the network must find, from the n neurons in the network, the neuron c such that

$$|E - M_c| = \min(|E - M_i|), \text{ with } 1 \leq i \leq n$$

In other words neuron c is selected because its weight vector M_c is the closest to the input vector E and is therefore the best representation of this input. Kohonen gives a proof that, normalising over the weight vectors and input vectors, this selection process identifies the neuron with the highest activation level for a particular associated input. This ensures that the activation level of each neuron is directly proportional to the 'resemblance' between the current input and the input for which that neuron was trained.

The second step in the learning process involves increasing the activation of the selected neuron, and the surrounding group of neurons, when this signal is presented. To take account of the lateral interaction between neurons it is now necessary to consider the neighbouring vectors to the selected neuron.

Kohonen proposed that a neighbourhood V_c, a circle centred on c, is defined around the neuron c selected by the comparison of weight vectors and input vectors. In the simplest form of lateral interaction, if neuron j lies within $V_c, S_j = 1$; if it lies outside $V_c, S_j = 0$. Taking the general form of the learning equation

$$\frac{dW_i}{dt} = kSe_i - \beta(S)W_i$$

The function $\beta(s) \geq 0$ is a function which implements forgetting; normally $k \geq 0$.

With the simplified values for S (0 or 1), $\beta(s)$ is chosen to be:

$$\beta(1) = k(t)$$
$$\beta(0) = 0$$

The learning rule that emerges is:

$$\frac{dW_{ij}}{dt} = \begin{cases} k(t)(E_j - W_{ij}) & \text{for neurons } i \text{ in } V_c \\ 0 & \text{for neurons } i \text{ outside } V_c \end{cases}$$

This rule is one of a number of possible models; others may be used. An incremental version of this learning algorithm is given in appendix B.

At this point in the presentation, it will be noted that the neighbourhood of a neuron c, V_c, used in the learning procedure, can be defined in different manners. The simulations carried out by Kohonen showed that it is best to choose this neighbourhood to be fairly large at the beginning of the learning process and to reduce its size during subsequent stages. Furthermore, considering different functions for $k(t)$, the most appropriate seem to be those functions which slowly decrease during the learning process. Most practically, $k(t)$ may be chosen as a function which linearly decreases with learning time, ensuring that learning terminates in finite time.

Different learning rules may be invented for different applications; the two degrees of freedom implicit in the auto-adaptive mechanisms are the method of identifying the appropriate neuron for a particular input and the way in which reinforcement of this neuron and its neighbours is carried out.

An example of simulating this type of network will show how the weight vectors tend to organise themselves into a set compatible with the topological relationships in the initial image set.

The network to be simulated is as described earlier in this section: a flat network, with a 10×10 matrix of neurons. The input vectors are two dimensional and can be represented as coordinates in a map.

The learning rule operates as described above, selecting, for each input vector, that neuron whose weights on connections to the inputs most closely match the vector itself.

In order to demonstrate the effects of learning, figures 5.8, 5.9, 5.10 and 5.11 depict four stages in the learning process, showing graphically the weights on the external connections of each of the neurons. Furthermore, to show the neighbourhood of each neuron, a line is drawn from the representation of each neuron point to each of its four neighbours.

The set of examples used consists of five hundred points chosen at random from a square plane. The diagrams clearly show the process of self-organisation operating in the network: this preserves the topological relationships of the training set inputs on the firing patterns of the neurons.

The maps shown in figures 5.8 to 5.11 were drawn following computer simulations carried out by D. Rakoto, a student at the Ecole Centrale de Paris.

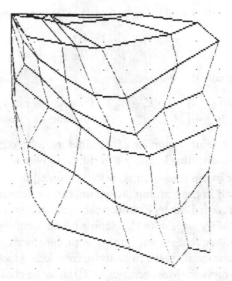

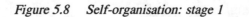

Figure 5.8   Self-organisation: stage 1

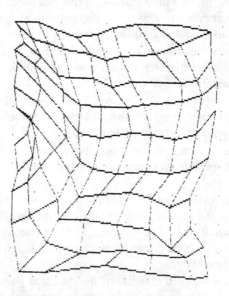

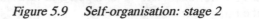

Figure 5.9   Self-organisation: stage 2

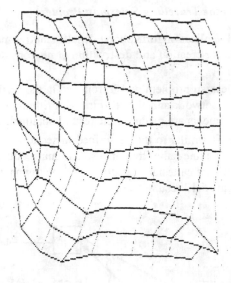

Figure 5.10   Self-organisation: stage 3

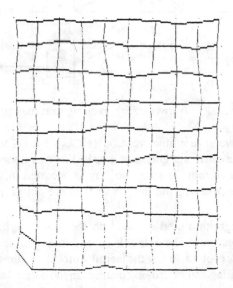

Figure 5.11   Self-organisation: stage 4

5.2.6   *Application to the Travelling Salesman Problem*

This problem is a new application for Kohonen's self-adaptive maps. Furthermore, an interesting process for creation and destruction of neurons during the learning phase is proposed.

The travelling salesman problem was introduced in the section describing the Hopfield model. The network and the learning algorithm are described in this section, and some comments are made on the results obtained.

The network used is similar to that described in section 5.2.5, except that its neurons are arranged in a line rather than in a square matrix on a plane. The input signals for this network are cartesian coordinates of the towns in the problem; the network shown in figure 5.12 results.

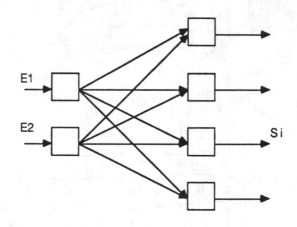

Figure 5.12   Network for travelling salesman problem

With n towns, we have n input vectors: $(E_1^i, E_2^i), 1 \le i \le n$. In the simulation, each neuron is represented on a graphical map by the (two-dimensional) coordinate given by its weight vectors. In the same way as occurred in section 5.2.5, if the neurons i and j are adjacent, the images of their weight vectors M_i and M_j are related.

The learning algorithm used is based on the following principles. Initially, there is only one neuron on the output layer and its vector of weights is the null vector. The network evolves during the learning process in three ways by changing weights and by creating and destroying neurons in the output layer. This evolution is carried out as the coordinates of different towns are successively presented, and its exact operation varies as the learning phase progresses.

In more detail, the modification of weights is carried out in the following manner: first, the neuron c whose weight vector is closest to the current input is selected. Secondly, the weight vector M_c and those of neurons in the neighbourhood

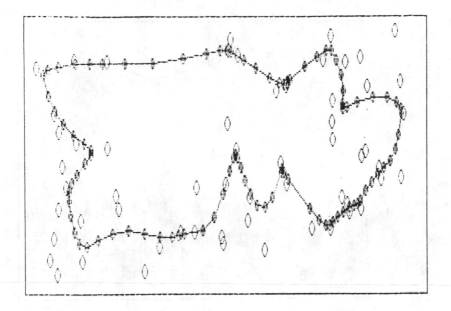

Figure 5.13   Travelling salesman: intermediate solution

of c are altered to make them closer to the input vector. The weights of neurons far from c are not modified. The scale of this modification and the size of neighbourhood c are both reduced as the learning stage progresses. For this problem the neurons at the two ends of the linear network are considered to be adjacent: in other words, the neurons form a loop.

Additional mechanisms are used for the creation and destruction of output neurons. A new neuron is created at the end of one learning iteration, over the full set of examples, if the same neuron was chosen to have its weights modified for two different towns. A neuron is destroyed if it is not selected in three successive iterations of learning over the full set of towns.

It apparent that as the evolutionary learning process progresses in the network, each neuron becomes associated with one town. Creation and destruction of neurons during the learning stage has two effects: it ensures that two neurons cannot be allocated to the same town and that two towns cannot correspond to the same neuron. This allows the size of the network to be adapted to the size of the problem, which is useful if the problem size is not known at the beginning of the learning stage or if the problem size changes subsequently.

As described above, each neuron is represented in the map by the image of its weight vector, which is related to the weights of the two neurons that are adjacent to it. Learning leads each weight vector to converge to the coordinates of one

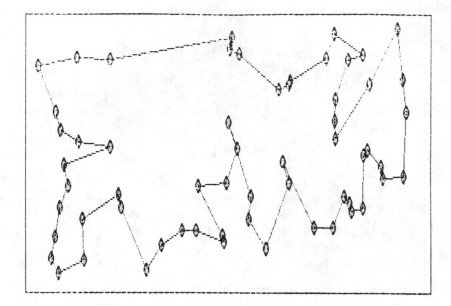

Figure 5.14   Travelling salesman: final solution

particular town so, at the end of the learning phase, each neuron has a map image which is the same as the location of the town with which it has become associated, by self-organisation. Looking at the map, then, gives one possible path which visits each town without visiting the same place twice, since each neuron image is connected only to two others. One initial constraint on the problem is implemented in this manner.

Consider the way in which the total journey length is minimised: the lateral interaction mechanism in the learning rule, tending to make the weight vectors of neighbouring neurons similar to each other, will also tend to minimise the distance between the image of these neighbourhood neurons, associating them with towns which are closest to each other. This leads the network to build shorter and shorter paths, connecting each town to its closest neighbours.

In conclusion, experimental results are very promising, showing both near optimal solutions to the problem, and use little computation time. Application of this method to other optimisation problems may need to wait until deeper theoretical studies have been carried out.

A complete version of the algorithm used here is given in appendix B; for further details of results see [Ang].

Figures 5.13 and 5.14 show the way in which this network develops, during training for a trip around towns distributed randomly on a map.

5.3 Adaptive Filters

5.3.1 Introduction

The networks described in this section can be described as filters with a transfer function F; they associate an input vector E to an output vector S, such that $S = F.E$ (in matrix notation).

These networks are called adaptive filters since their parameters may change as a function of signals which they process. For each input signal, the network provides an initial response, and then continues to evolve until it reaches a stable state.

The mechanisms used in this model essentially depend on the interconnections between different neurons in the network and the dynamic stability properties of the system.

First, the overall structure of these networks is described in detail; different rules of operation are then proposed and commented upon.

5.3.2 Network Description

Again, the general model presented in section 5.1 is followed, but it is modified in the following manner. First, the weight vector is initialised: $M = I$, where I is the identity matrix. This means that each neuron is connected to one single input cell and the weight of this connection is 1. In order to use familiar notations we say that $N = W$ and the activation function of each neuron is defined to be linear:

$$S_i = e_i + \sum_j W_{ij} S_j$$

The number of neurons in the network is given by n, $1 \leq j \leq n$. We therefore obtain the schema shown in figure 5.15 with state equations given by

$$
\begin{aligned}
S &= E + W.S &(1)\\
M &= I &(2)\\
\frac{dW}{dt} &= H(S, W) &(3)
\end{aligned}
$$

To derive the transfer function, we set: $F = (I - w)^{-1}$, which allows equation 1 to be written $S = F.E$.

Equations 1 and 2 may be solved conventionally; it only remains to ponder on the different possibilities for equation 3, which determines the specific behaviour of this network.

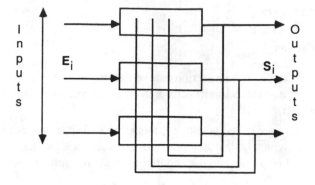

Figure 5.15   Adaptive filter network

5.3.3 A Self-associative Memory

In this model, rule 3 is simply the Hebb rule. Here the same learning rule is used as that encountered in the Hopfield model:

$$\frac{dW}{dt} = k.S.S^t, \text{ with } k \geq 0 \quad (3)$$

The forgetting term is omitted both to simplify the model and because a mathematical result, described in [Koh], shows that long term stability is ensured if connection weights vary little over short periods.

A solution for F is obtained by manipulating and simplifying the state equations:

$$F(t) = I + k \int^t E(t').E^t(t')dt'$$

Here $E(t')$ is the input of the network at time t' and $E^t(t')$ is the transpose of the E vector.

If the input vector changes at each time step, remaining constant during a time step, and K inputs are presented, $E^1, E^2, \ldots, E^K$, the transfer function becomes:

$$F = I + k \sum_{l=1,K} E^l.E^{lt}$$

In this expression, $E^l.E^{lt}$ is the auto-correlation matrix of vector E^l.

If a new vector E is presented to the network, the output is given by:

$$S = F.E = E + k \sum_{l=1,K} (E^{lt}.E).E^l$$

This may also be written as:

$$S = E + \sum_{l=1,K}(\mu_l E^l)$$

Interpretation

If the internal connections between neurons are ignored, the network gives simply $S = E$. The term $\sum_{l=1,K}(\mu_l E^l)$ therefore represents the contribution of internal connections to the network's ou put vector, a contribution which is a weighted sum of the inputs that have previously been learned.

The term $E^{lt}.E$ represents a measure of the similarity between E and E^{lt}. If E and E^{lt} are orthogonal, this term is zero; it takes its maximum value when they are identical. The dominant term in the sum $\sum_{l=1,K}(\mu_l E^l)$ is therefore the vector within E^l which is the 'closest' to E.

Conclusion

In the response of the network to an input E, the term which dominates is that which is the most similar to E; this mechanism can be used to find messages which have been deformed or altered, such as the case in character recognition. This type of network can therefore be considered for use as a self-associative memory.

There is, nevertheless, a significant limitation on the performance of this network. If the learning vectors are not orthogonal to each other, when a vector that has already been learned is presented the network gives a response that is altered by the correlations between the different input vectors previously learned. To avoid this problem, we need a preprocessing method which allows the input vectors to be made orthogonal.

Kohonen proposes two radically different ways of carrying this out. One involves spatial differentiation; the other involves the use of multiple networks, two being exposed simultaneously to an input. This allows the input vectors to be preprocessed to give orthogonal outputs.

If the input vectors are all orthogonal with each other, the matrix $\sum_{l=1,K}(E^l.E^{lt})$ is the orthogonal projection matrix over the subspace given by the vectors E^l.

5.3.4 A Filter for Detecting Novelty

For this application, the form of equation 3 becomes:

$$\frac{dW}{dt} = -kS.S^t, \text{ with } k \geq 0 \quad (3)$$

The principal characteristic of this operating rule is that if the same input vector is continuously applied to the network, the output of the network tends towards 0.

The behaviour of this network can be related to results from experimental psychology; the phenomenon of 'habituation' occurs in both natural and synthetic systems. This type of adaptation appears in the visual system, for example: the strength of response to a signal diminishes progressively if the signal is continuously applied.

Initially, the memory of this network is empty; $W(0) = 0$. Consider a finite set of vectors $E^1, \ldots, E^k$. Mathematically, it can be shown that if each of these examples is presented for an infinite time to the network, the matrix F will converge to a projection matrix, such that for all i belonging to the set $\{1 \ldots K\}$, $F.E^i = 0$. Thus any input vector E which is a linear combination of vectors from the learning set has the property that $F.E = 0$. Conversely, if an input vector does not belong to the subspace described by the vectors learned, $F.E \neq 0$. F is the orthogonal projector over subspaces orthogonal to the subspace defined by the vectors that were learned.

In practical terms, it is not possible to consider infinite times; instead, it is sufficient to present the different input vectors only for sufficiently long times that the transfer function obtained is a good approximation to the asymptotic function. The function F that is finally obtained is an approximation of the projection matrix, always ensuring that $F.E^i = 0$ for i belonging to the set $\{1 \ldots K\}$.

Note that if the state equation had contained a term to implement forgetting, it would have become:

$$\frac{dW}{dt} = -kS.S^t - \beta W, \text{ with } k \geq 0 \text{ and } \beta \geq 0 \quad (3)$$

The solution for F would have had the same form as that found without using the forgetting term.

Commentary

This type of network is called a novelty detector for the following reasons: if the input vector applied to the network has already been learned, the response is the null vector; the filter is said to be 'opaque' for the vectors that are learned. When a new vector is applied to the network, before the network adapts itself to the new input, using rule 3, the initial output represents what is novel to the network, by reference to signals that it has already learned. The output of the network corresponds to a transformation carried out on that part of the input vector which is not a linear combination of vectors already learned.

For an input E, which is a combination of a known input E^a and an unknown input E^b, we have:

$$E = E^a + E^b, \text{ with } E^a = \sum_{l=1,K} c_l.E_l \text{ and } E^a \text{ orthogonal to } E^b$$

The output obtained is given by $F.E = F.E^a + F.E^b = F.E^b$.

Conclusion

This type of filter can be used to reveal anomalies, on radiographic medical images, for example, since it allows parts missing or supplementary parts to be shown, even if at the start of learning it is not possible to specify which parts are 'normally' present in these images.

5.3.5 Projective Filters

Sections 5.3.3 and 5.3.4 showed that the filters considered acted as projective functions.

In the case of section 5.3.3, when the vectors to be learned are orthogonal to each other, the transfer function may be written $F = I + aP$, where P is the orthogonal projection over the subspace defined by the vectors to be memorised.

In the case of section 5.3.4, an input vector could be written as $E = E^a + E^b$ where E^a is the orthogonal projection of E over the subspace defined by the vectors that have been learned. The network output is therefore $FE = FE^b$, where E^b is orthogonal to the subspace defined by the training vectors:

$$FE = E - E^a = E^b$$

The advantage of projective functions arises from their ability to 'improve' input vectors, by making them closer to input vectors that are already learned. When a vector E, a noisy version of a vector E^l which is already learned, is presented to the network, the result is E^a which is the orthogonal projection of E over the subspace defined by the vectors already learned. Kohonen showed that E^a is therefore a better approximation than E.

In the same way, if considering the case described in section 5.3.4, E^b may be considered as a better approximation of the novel features of the vector E, comparing it against vectors that have already been learned by the network.

5.3.6 The General Case

In the most general case, we wish to construct a filter, a self-associative or heteroassociative memory, which associates a set of input vectors E^l to a set of output vectors S^l using a transfer function F:

$$F.E^l = S^l, \text{ with } 1 \leq l \leq K$$

The optimal linear solution is given by a method defined by Penrose: let $X = [E^1, \ldots, E^K]$ and $Y = [S^1, \ldots, S^K]$;

$$F.E^l = S^l, \text{ with } 1 \leq l \leq K; \text{ written } F.X = Y$$

The optimal solution is $F = Y.X^+$, where X^+ is the pseudo-inverse of X. An algorithm for calculating X^+ is given in appendix B.

It is worth noting that if the vectors E^l are orthogonal, $Y.X^+ = Y.X^t$, and an exact solution of the system $F.X = Y$ is given by $F = Y.X^t$. In this case, the solution of section 5.3.3 is re-encountered.

5.4 Pattern Recognition

5.4.1 Introduction

Pattern recognition can be defined as a process which leads to a decision. The quality of this decision can only be measured by statistics relating the number of 'good' and 'bad' classifications.

Kohonen's goal was to construct a system which, following a supervised learning stage, would be capable of classifying shapes with a minimum number of errors.

To carry out this task, he used his general network model, simplifying it and taking note of the set-backs encountered when applying 'classical' neural network models in this problem domain.

5.4.2 Classical Network Limitations

According to Kohonen, the classical models of neural networks, the perceptron, for example, are limited in their performance on difficult problems in pattern recognition, such as speech recognition, by the inadequacies in their learning criterion and their classification criterion.

For example, the classification criterion for a particular input may simply be related to its position with respect to a frontier between two or more decision spaces. The learning criterion used in classical networks tries to ensure a correct value for each response, a value independent of the position of the input with respect to the frontiers of its class. This may explain why their results are sometimes poorer than those of Bayesian classifiers, which attempt to optimise their decision surfaces.

Kohonen presents a model differing from perceptron networks in the following three ways: first, only the reference weight vector closest to the input is modified. Secondly the modification is carried out both for correct classifications and for erroneous classifications; and finally the correction procedure is numerically compatible with the criteria used for identification.

5.4.3 Algorithm Description

The general network model is simplified since it does not include interconnections between the neurons of the network. Each input is always connected to all neurons in the network. To improve the classification performance of the network, it seems preferable to have a number of outputs active for one class rather than just one specific neuron. Neurobiological justifications for the learning algorithm described below are given in [Koh].

For each neuron i, W_i is the vector of weights on connections coming from the input signal. If the input signal is of dimension n, $W_i = W_{i_1}, \ldots, W_{i_n}$. The number of neurons is significantly higher than the number of classes so that several neurons can be associated with one class. For training, a set of examples E exists: $E^l, 1 \leq l \leq K$.

$$E^l = (E^l_1, \ldots, E^l_n)$$

For each example in the training set, the class that it belongs to is known.

The supervised learning algorithm (defined mathematically in appendix B) is as follows: each class has allocated a number of neurons proportional to the *a priori* probability, derived from the set of training examples, of this class occurring. The weight vectors are initialised with the first available examples; each weight vector takes the value of an input vector drawn from the appropriate class of input.

Once each neuron is associated with a class, a procedure for modification of the neuron weights ensues. Each time a new example E is presented, it is compared to the full set of weight vectors and the weight W_c, closest to the vector E, is selected and processed in the following manner. If the input example belongs to the class allotted to c, W_c is modified to make it closer to E. If the example does not belong to the class allotted to neuron c, the weight W_c is altered to be more distant from E. No modification of the weights of other neurons takes place.

Once the learning phase is finished, a vector E presented to the network causes it to search for the neuron with the closest weight vectors; this neuron then represents the class to which the example presented belongs.

Results obtained with this model are very close to results from Bayesian classifiers.

5.5 Summary

The Kohonen model may be summarised as follows:

$S = (S_1, \ldots, S_i, \ldots, S_n)$ is the output vector of the n neurons in the network;

$E = (E_1, \ldots, E_i, \ldots, E_m)$ is the input vector from the m external inputs;

M is the matrix of connection weights from external inputs to the neurons;

N is the matrix of weights on the connections between neurons in the network.

$$\frac{dS}{dt} = F(E, S, M, N) \quad (1)$$

$$\frac{dM}{dt} = G(E, S, M) \quad (2)$$

$$\frac{dN}{dt} = H(S, N) \quad (3)$$

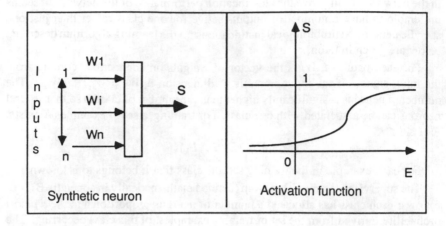

Figure 5.16   The Kohonen neuron

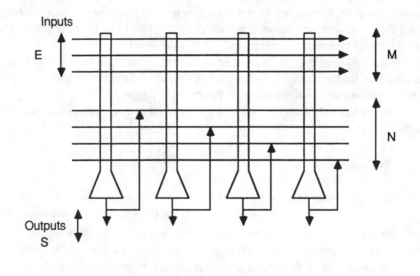

Figure 5.17   Network architecture

Conclusion

The Kohonen model is distinguished by two characteristics, self-adaptation and projection. The form of auto-adaptation that he proposed means that the topological shape of the neuron activation map is similar to the shape of input signals. Among other benefits, this feature enables the creation of preprocessing or orthogonalisation modules for problems in pattern recognition.

The projection carried out by Kohonen filters permits their use for data compression and ensures that they have a high noise resistance, when used as auto- or hetero-associative memories.

6 Applications of Neural Networks

In previous chapters, the principal models used in neural networks have been introduced; it is now appropriate to describe their applications, some real and some potential.

6.1 Introduction

We start by summarising the specific properties of neural networks responsible for the interest that they arouse today. Introducing the limitations of today's neural techniques leads to a definition of the characteristics of suitable applications, allowing definition of a number of different domains within the overall field of applications of neural networks.

This analysis permits a methodology for their use to be derived, using a general review of application domains for neural networks, descriptions of some implementations and concluding with a detailed description of one application.

6.2 Reasons for Using Neural Networks

6.2.1 Some Fascinating Properties

The general interest in neural networks today arises from their fascinating properties which enable them to exceed the limitations of traditional information processing, such as the need for detailed programming.

Amongst these properties are their parallelism, their capacity for adaptation, and their use of distributed memory, all of which arise directly from modelling features of the human nervous system.

Furthermore, a capacity for generalisation emerges from a study of the operation of neural networks. In the study of the brain, this property corresponds to a higher, psychological level of interpretation of the brain's operation. Finally, from an operational point of view, applications using neural networks may be developed or simulated with some degree of simplicity.

Parallelism

Parallelism is fundamental in the architecture of neural networks when these are considered as sets of elementary units operating simultaneously. This parallelism in data processing is interesting because of the limitations of sequential methods of processing large problems needing an enormous quantity of data, sometimes giving rise to a combinatorial explosion in processing requirements. Through the use of parallel hardware, parallelism allows a greatly increased speed of calculation, but demands that problems to be resolved are stated, and thought of in a different, unconventional manner. Studying the operation of neural networks, which are intrinsically parallel, may give insights into new techniques of specifying other problems, allowing these to be tackled in parallel.

Capacity for Adaptation

This property of neural networks first manifests itself in their ability to learn, which allows networks to take account of new constraints or new data from the external world as they arise. Furthermore, it appears in certain networks by their capacity to self-organise, ensuring their stability as dynamic systems.

This capacity for adaptation is particularly relevant for problems which evolve; these need to take account of situations which are not yet known in order to resolve problems. This may mean that the network is able to take account of a change in the problem that it is solving, or that it may learn to resolve the problem in a new manner.

Distributed Memory

In neural networks 'memory' corresponds to an activation map of the neurons; this map is in some ways a coding of facts that are stored. Memory is thus distributed over many units, giving a valuable property, resistance to noise.

In the first place, the loss of one individual component does not necessarily cause the loss of a stored data item. This is different from the case of a traditional computer, in which individual data is stored in individual memory units, and in which the loss of one memory unit causes its data to be lost permanently. In a neural network the destruction of one memory unit only marginally changes the activation map of the neurons.

Secondly, when one atomic piece of knowledge corresponds to one piece of data stored in a particular place, the problem of managing the full set of knowledge arises. In order to find or to use one particular fact, it is necessary to know precisely either its address or its contents. This technique cannot therefore take account of noisy data and preprocessing of data must therefore be used to eliminate the noise.

This limitation is overcome in distributed memories such as neural networks, in which it is possible to start with noisy data and to make the correct data appear from the network's activation map without noise.

Capacity for Generalisation

The capacity for generalisation of neural networks was demonstrated by the example of learning the forms of the past tense for English verbs, introduced in chapter 3 in the context of back-propagation.

This capability is crucial; its importance has been shown in recent years by the difficulty of acquiring rules for expert systems. Many problems are solved by experts in a more or less intuitive manner, making it very difficult to state explicitly the knowledge base and the rules which are necessary for its exploitation.

It is therefore highly significant to consider a system which may learn the rules simply from a set of examples, or which may learn to mimic a behaviour, allowing the problem itself to be solved.

Ease of Construction

Computer simulation of a neural network for a small example is simple and requires only a short development time. For more complex applications, simulators or accelerator cards have proved useful. Some simulators are now extremely easy to use.

6.2.2 Limits in the Use of Neural Networks

The list of attractive properties of neural networks needs to be tempered by considering the principal limitations on their use.

First, there is the operational problem encountered when attempting to simulate the parallelism of neural networks. The majority of networks are simulated on sequential machines, giving rise to a very rapid increase in processing time requirements as the size of the problem grows. This is particularly true when simulating networks which use Boltzmann machines or those which use back-propagation.

Steps are being made to implement neural networks directly in hardware, but these are in their infancy. This process will enable the true exploitation of the network's parallelism, but may lose much of the flexibility of software simulations.

Faced with these problems, the principal applications proposed for neural networks have been on a modest scale. A current act of faith is that if present techniques allow neural networks to solve fairly small problems, technological evolution will permit much larger problems to be addressed in the future.

The requirement for preprocessing data is also a difficult point currently unresolved. One of the advantages of neural networks is often to minimise the importance associated with preprocessing; however, their performance may be very sensitive to the quality and the type of any preprocessing.

Finally, one of the most significant limitations of neural networks is their inability to explain any results that they obtain. Networks operate as 'black boxes' whose rules of operation are completely unknown. The quality of their performance can therefore only be measured by statistical methods, which may give rise to a certain distrust on the part of their potential users.

6.2.3 Characteristics of Suitable Applications

Following these general descriptions some of the characteristics of problems which are suitable for implementation on neural networks may be described.

The rules used in solving the problem may be unknown or very difficult to explain or formalise. Instead of these rules a set of examples exists, giving a set of inputs to the problem and their corresponding solutions, given by experts.

The problem makes use of noisy data.

The problem may evolve, for example by varying its set of initial conditions.

The problem may need very high speed processing: processing in real time, for example.

There may be no current technical solutions.

These constraints suggest a possible list of application domains: pattern recognition, signal processing, vision, speech processing, forecasting and modelling, decision making aids and robotics. These different applications exhibit most of the characteristics described above; many studies of the applications of neural networks have addressed problems in these domains.

In addition, neural networks may play a significant role as instruments of simulation in the study of the brain; active work is also progressing in research into neuro-computers and new computer architectures.

6.3 Methodology

The methodology for using neural networks in novel applications consists of two stages. The first involves a study of the problem, determining its suitability for solution using neural networks, and defining the objectives to be addressed, enabling the quality of the solution obtained to be assessed. The second applies the methods of neural networks, involving the choice of a particular network type and its implementation as a function of the characteristics of the individual problem and the user's objectives.

6.3.1 Step One

For a problem to be suitable for solution by neural networks, the problem must exhibit the characteristics described in section 6.2.3 and must possess a large number of data points, enabling learning to take place and the performance of the network to be verified. Next, the nature of the data must be considered to determine

whether preprocessing is necessary; finally, the size of the problem must be determined and the possibility of dividing it into sub-problems considered if necessary.
At this stage the desired performance is defined, both for the learning phase and
for production use.

6.3.2   Step Two

The choice of the type of network and its type of implementation is based on the
nature of the application, the nature of the data and performance considerations.
The table contained in figure 6.1 gives an indication of the types of network suitable for different applications.

Application	Network model			
	Back-propagation	Hopfield	Boltzmann machine	Kohonen
Classification	•	•	•	•
Image processing	•			•
Decision-making	•		•	•
Optimisation		•	•	•

Figure 6.1   Current applications areas for different neural networks

6.4   Review of Different Applications

In this section, two different classification schemes for potential applications of
neural networks are presented; certain implementations used to date are then described.

6.4.1   Classification by Sectors of Activity

A number of sectors may be defined: industrial, financial, telecommunications and
environmental.

Industrial Applications

Quality control, production planning and material planning, fault diagnosis, com-
bining data from several sources.

Financial Sector

Prediction and modelling of markets (chartism), signature analysis, automatic
reading of handwritten characters (cheques), applying credits, selection of invest-
ments.

Telecommunications Sector

Signal analysis, noise elimination, data compression.

Environment Sector

Risk evaluation, chemical analysis, weather forecasting, resource management.

6.4.2   *Classification by Application Domain*

The same essential types of problem occur many times in both applied research and real applications: pattern recognition, signal processing, adaptive control, vision and speech, forecasting and modelling, optimisation and the management of information.

Finally, neural networks are highly valued in research into the structure of the nervous system and its operation.

6.4.3   *Application Examples*

Pattern Recognition

Neural networks have, since their very earliest days, been applied to pattern recognition. The general term 'pattern recognition' describes a process which operates on data to extract information in order to classify the data. Pattern recognition is used for different applications including character recognition, of both handwritten and printed characters, weather forecasting, the analysis of financial trends and biomedical imaging. A neural network for the recognition of postal codes was implemented by the Nestor Company using its simulator NDS. They used a set of 9,000 handwritten characters, divided into a training set of 7,200 characters and a test set of 1,800 characters. The characters were preprocessed to encode them according to nine characteristics. The performance of this network, when it was allowed to reject characters about which it was uncertain, reached 97.7% correct recognitions.

Signal Processing

In this area, neural networks have been used to recognise radar or sonar signatures.

The same company, Nestor, have developed a neural network which identified a target with 100% certainty and recognised random noise with a success rate of 95%. This application was constructed using sonar signals, encoding features of the signal found by experts to be useful in identifying a target in a noisy environment. In this application the network is used as a filter to eliminate noise.

Adaptive Control

This domain includes robotics and quality control as well as other applications.

A network was devised by Barto, Sutton and Anderson [Bar], to control the stability of an inverted pendulum mounted on a trolley, shown in figure 6.2.

The trolley and pendulum can only move in the vertical plane on the diagram, and the trolley is free to move between two end points. The system is thus characterised by the following data; the position of the trolley, the angle of the pendulum from vertical, the speed of the trolley and the angular velocity of the pendulum. This data is digitised and input to the network, which can reply in one of two ways, exerting a force on the trolley either towards the left or the right. In less than 100 test sessions, the network was capable of learning how to keep the pendulum upright on the trolley.

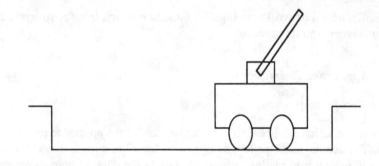

Figure 6.2   The inverted pendulum

Speech and Vision

Applications using neural networks have been developed for both recognition and synthesis of speech. NETTalk, developed by Sejnowski and Rosenberg [Sej], a neural network which learns to speak out loud texts written in English, was described in an earlier section.

This type of problem is particularly well adapted to solution using neural networks, as English pronunciation follows a number of rules, each with exceptions and modifications. This example shows how neural networks cope with problems which involve statistical regularities, without being confused by exceptions.

NETTalk operates by reading strings of characters forming a complete English text and converting them into strings of phonemes which act as the input to a voice synthesiser.

The researchers used a network with three layers. Two learning algorithms were tested: the Boltzmann machine algorithm and the back-propagation algorithm. The results given by these two algorithms were very similar, but back-propagation showed a rather quicker learning characteristic.

The input layer consisted of 203 (7 x 29) neurons. A character window, 7 characters wide, was used to slide over the text with one position per character. The number of different characters considered, including spaces and punctuation, was 29. The hidden layer consisted of 80 neurons and the output layer 26, which acted as a coding of the different phonemes.

After a dozen cpu hours of learning, on a DEC Vax computer, NETTalk was capable of producing phonemes from the learning text with a success rate of 95%. Other examples from outside the training text gave a success rate of 80%. After the learning stage, NETTalk was comprehensible to the human listener, in spite of the errors it made.

Other applications have been addressed in the domain of vision processing, in particular by the Nestor company again. They have developed neural networks capable of recognising objects in three dimensions in real time.

Forecasting and Modelling

This type of application of neural networks increasingly attracts non-specialist users, professionals from the worlds of finance or insurance in particular, since models of financial markets using expert systems or mathematical models have not been particularly successful. Recourse to neural networks offers a promising path but this area is in its infancy and has a number of problems, both practical and theoretical.

One financial application worth describing was implemented by Bailey, Thompson and Feinstein [Bai]. Their paper describes a study of shares of the Merck Company and call options on these shares. (A call option is the right to acquire a given quantity of shares at a fixed price, called the exercise price, at a fixed future date.)

The Merck company shares were chosen for their price stability and their trading volume; furthermore, its call options are widely traded and have a variety of expiry dates.

The aim of the application was to predict the optimal moment to exercise the call option, based on a prediction of its price movements. The network was to output the trend and a prediction of the price of the call options.

Tests carried out on different types of network showed that the back-propagation model was best adapted to this application. The best network consisted of 12 input neurons, 9 in a hidden layer and 2 output neurons. The output neurons indicated the desired trend and a prediction of the option price. Difficulties were encountered during the training phase due to the presence of local minima, but these were overcome by common techniques. During this phase, each example was presented 1,000 times. The best network gave correct results more than 90% of the time on the test data; using data outside the test set, the precision fell to 80%.

The data input to the network was as follows: the price of the option, its volatility, the price of the share, the number of shares traded, the exercise price, the expiry time, the current interest rate and a prediction of future interest rates. Each data value was normalised to lie within the range -0.5 to 0.5.

The simulation was carried out on a PC using the ANSIM Program from ASIC.

In conclusion, the predictive abilities of this application were found to be better than those of statistical systems. This application has not got beyond the prototype stage because of the problems of confidence and trust. Perhaps a natural development would be to couple this system to an expert system in order to automate the processing of market information.

Finally, it is worth noting that the market in share options is fairly well understood and well modelled today; perhaps it would be interesting to investigate the use of neural networks in the market in bond options or to predict interest rates.

Optimisation

Following the description of Hopfield models of simulated annealing and of the Kohonen model, it is unnecessary to repeat an explanation of the full value of neural networks in problems which suffer combinatorial explosion. The best known example of these problems is the travelling salesman problem. A similar type of solution has been used to resolve scheduling problems, such as that involving the distribution of tasks in a library [Goy].

This application attempts to solve the problem of organising the reclassification of volumes in a library, knowing that each librarian is more or less effective in classification, depending upon subject matter. The goal of the problem is to maximise the overall speed of operation of the team.

This type of problem is found in every organisation involving teams of workers.

Simulations carried out on a Vax 780 computer gave very good results within a few tens of seconds, for a total of 30 people.

Information Management

The problems that arise in the management of large databases, especially those which attempt to provide general archival search facilities, which can be customised for the needs of each different user, have not been well addressed, either by classical computer techniques, or by expert systems. Here we describe an implementation of Cochet and Paget [Coc] which uses a connectionist approach to improve the construction of a database full of images and its search mechanisms.

The network used is divided into two parts, one consisting of neurons which represent each of the stored images, the other of neurons representing the descriptions of the stored images. These serve as features to the user, allowing the images

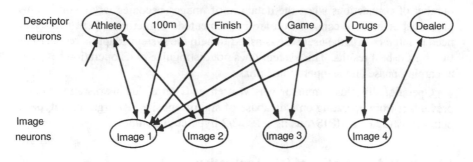

Figure 6.3   Managing an image library

to be retrieved to be characterised. The two types of neurons are shown in figure 6.3.

The network operates in the following manner: when a user wishes to enter a new image, he creates a neuron in the image neuron layer and connects it either to existing descriptor neurons or to new descriptor neurons, created specifically to describe this image. These connections are symmetric and are effected by small synaptic weights. Figure 6.4 shows the network after a new image has been introduced.

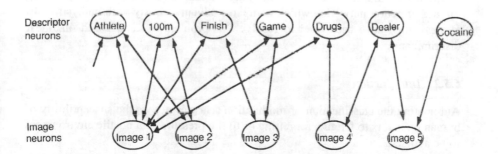

Figure 6.4   Managing an image library - adding an image

This process allows each user to organise his own set of images.

In order to retrieve an image, the user provides to the system a list of descriptors and a measure of their relevance. The neurons which correspond to these descriptors are then activated, proportionately to the relevance of these descriptors and the value of their activation is allowed to flow through the network connections. After a certain number of diffusion steps, both forward and backward diffusion taking place, the system selects those images which are represented by the image neurons whose activation is the strongest.

In order to avoid an explosion in the number of descriptor neurons and in the number of connections when the database of images becomes large, continuous processes of internal construction are implemented. Sometimes these processes need to interact with the user who is asked to help the system adapt its reconstruction for the best results. This system does not distinguish in its operation between a learning phase and an operational phase.

Operationally, this simulator was written in C on a Sun workstation which prevents it from operating on a database of significant size. A larger prototype is being constructed by IRISA using a IPSC/2 hypercube computer.

6.5   Detailed Description of One Application

6.5.1   Overview

The subject of this application is the automatic identification of the transmission mode of a data transmission, received by radio communication. This is a problem which occurs frequently in the civil domain, in a regulatory organisation which must be capable of controlling radio communications, and in the military domain where encoded methods of transmission make counter-methods more and more difficult. Even experienced personnel may frequently not be able to classify signals in real time, especially if the signals are unfamiliar and use different modulation schemes.

In this section, we describe the computer simulation of classification based on the use of neural networks, which compares advantageously with analysis techniques which have been used to resolve this problem to date, based on linear discriminants.

6.5.2   Introduction

Automating the classification of modulation schemes allows the susceptibility of human operators to fatigue, forgetting or to the pressure of a hostile environment to be avoided.

The modulations to be considered are as follows: amplitude modulation with suppressed carrier (AM), frequency modulation (FREQ), single side band modulation (SSB), binary phase modulation (BPSK), quadrature phase modulation (QPSK) and binary frequency modulation (BFSK). To this list, random noise is added, giving seven different classes to be distinguished. All of these modulation schemes, including noise, are simulated by computer for the purposes of training and evaluation.

The application is a classical pattern recognition problem, divided into two significant phases. Firstly, a signal processing phase involves preprocessing the signal to extract the signatures of the modulations in question. This phase represents the data acquisition phase. Secondly, a classification phase operates on the preprocessed data.

6.5.3 Data Acquisition

The unknown received signal is preprocessed before presentation to the neural network; it is supposed that the frequency band within which the signal is transmitted is known.

Preprocessing recovers the sampled complex envelope of the signal, the set of real and imaginary values sampled. This gives us a set of complex values $x_n = a_n \exp(ip_n)$. A set of features are extracted from these values; the features are amplitude, frequency and the instantaneous phase:

$$a_n, (p_n - p_{n-1})/f_e, p_n \ (f_e \text{ is the sampling frequency})$$

From the set of values of these three variables, histograms are constructed, forming the signatures of each modulation scheme and of random noise.

Operationally, the amplitude modulated signals, frequency modulated signals and SSB signals were simulated using a real speech signal with a duration of 3 seconds, sampled at 8 kHz; the DPSK, BFSK and QPSK modulations were derived using a random sequence of bits. This gave a sample file for each of these modulation schemes with around 23,000 data points.

Each of these simulated signals was subjected to noise with different levels of signal to noise ratio, 5 dB, 15 dB and 30 dB, successively decreasing the noise. Files containing the value of the three variables, amplitude, frequency and phase were obtained from these noise-treated, sampled modulated signals. The full set of examples was derived by dividing each original file into six parts; each resulting file contained 4,000 values and therefore represented a real signal with a duration of 0.5 second.

Before proceeding to a description of the classification stage, note that we have six files for each modulation scheme, for each level of noise corruption and six files of pure noise, for each of the three variables. In total, we have 114 files which make up the set of examples to be recognised automatically.

6.5.4 Construction of the Classifier

A classical technique, using a linear discriminator to classify different histograms, consists of projecting the histograms considered as vectors in N dimensions (if there are N cases) onto a subspace of dimension n (if there are n classes to differentiate) in such a way that the projection matrix, constructed from the examples whose class is known, associates components of a particular class to exactly one of the vectors from the canonical base set.

These techniques, which have been used previously to resolve this problem, showed very acceptable performance with signal-to-noise ratios better than 15 dB, but degrade significantly as soon as more noisy signals are introduced.

For this reason we considered that the use of neural networks in this problem might be of interest. We simulated a number of three-layer networks using the back-propagation algorithm as their learning rule. To improve control over the learning process, we decided to dedicate one network to each of the three signal variables (amplitude, frequency and phase); since one single variable does not suffice to distinguish between all modulation types, we then constructed a rudimentary logic system to use a function of the results coming from the three individual networks to determine the modulation type of a received signal.

The construction and validation of the networks took place in four stages: the choice of inputs of the networks, that is the construction of the learning histograms from the available example files, the choice of outputs of the network, that is the choice of discriminant classes for each variable and their encoding, the choice of overall architecture for the three networks designed, and finally, tests on the networks using new sampled data. It is apparent that the first three phases proceeded simultaneously, rather than independently.

Choice of Inputs

Three operations were carried out on each of the example files: normalisation, to bring all of the values into the interval (0,1), the construction of histograms to quantify these sets of normalised values, and normalisation of these histograms to bring them into values in the interval (0,1).

The normalisation operations were carried out to cope with variations in transmission power and to adapt the values of the histograms to input neurons of the networks. Each element in the histogram is connected to a single input neuron of the network, taking values between 0 and 1.

The choice of quantising unit was selected following a visual evaluation of each individual variable over the set of examples, represented graphically. Tests were conducted quantising into 16 or 32 values, depending on the variable considered.

Choice of Outputs

In the same way, the choice of outputs was determined visually. We decided to make the neural networks attempt to carry out classifications that we were able to perform using the naked eye on the histograms, without the aid or the advice of an expert in detecting modulation type. Other solutions were tried but none gave results as good. This process gave rise to the following classifications. For the instantaneous frequency variable, five classes were distinguished: AM, SSB, FM or Noise, QPSK, and BPSK or BFSK. For the amplitude variable, three classes are distinguished, AM or SSB, Noise, and BFSK or BPSK or QPSK or FM. For the instantaneous phase variable, four classes are differentiated, AM, QPSK, BPSK, and Noise or FM or SSB or BFSK.

Different encoding of outputs did not give rise to significant performance differences and we decided to associate one class with each output neuron and vice versa.

Overall Choice of Architecture

Experiments carried out in the learning phase led us to use the three following networks: for the instantaneous frequency variable we used 32 input neurons, 18 neurons in the hidden layer, and 5 output neurons. We considered learning complete after 340 presentations of each of the training set of examples to the network.

For the amplitude variable we used 16 input neurons, 9 hidden layer neurons and 3 output neurons. Learning was completed after 150 presentations of each example. With a network having 32 neurons as input learning was always prevented by local minima. At this stage, a visual examination of the histograms led us to hypothesise that quantising them into 32 cases was too fine a division and prevented the characteristic features of groups of modulation from standing out.

For the instantaneous phase variable we used 32 input neurons, 15 hidden neurons, and 4 output neurons. Learning was complete after each examples was presented 500 times to the network. In order to arrive at this result, we needed to modify the order of presentation of examples during the learning phase; at 5 dB signal-to-noise ratio it was impossible to distinguish a histogram of amplitude modulation from a histogram of BPSK. This was consistent with the fact that it is practically impossible for a non-expert to distinguish between the two histograms by eye. The order of presentation of the example set was modified following the simple observation that, taking account of the available examples and the classes to be distinguished, the class consisting of the FM, SSB, BFSK and Noise modulations appeared four times more frequently than the others, which were not learned at all by the network. To get over this difficulty, the number of examples presented for each class of desired output was evened out.

For all of these networks, learning was considered as complete when the maximum error, measured over all of the output neurons, between the desired and the obtained value was less than 0.1, for an arbitrary input from the training set. The last network is slightly different since, as described above, confusion existed between AM and BPSK modulations at 5 dB signal-to-noise ratio. The network completely satisfied the learning criteria for other modulations with other levels of noise.

Finally, we note that the size of the networks considered shows that it is feasible to consider using this technique in a real-time environment.

Tests Carried Out on the Classifier

After the learning phase, we tested a system, consisting of the three neural networks and a simple logic decision circuit, with new signals which covered the same types of modulation with noise levels varying from 5 dB to 30 dB signal-to-noise ratio, but which could be different from the three individual levels used in the learning phase.

We obtained a recognition rate of 100% for AM, SSB and QPSK modulation at noise levels of 5, 10, 15 and 30 dB. Noise was also recognised 100% correctly. There were two cases of confusion: between FM and BPSK modulation and between FM and BFSK modulation. These confusions only arrived when the signal-to-noise ratio fell to 5 dB, and the presence of either BFSK or BPSK was detected with 98% success rate notwithstanding this error.

6.5.5 Conclusion

The best human experts can operate on signals with signal-to-noise ratio of 5 dB; this is three times better than the 15 dB ratio given by classical methods.

This study, carried out over a very short period of time, shows that neural networks can be very effective in certain problems in pattern recognition, even when real-time operational constraints are imposed upon the problem.

From a practical point of view on neural networks, the problems that emerged during the learning phase serve to re-emphasise a couple of drawbacks. The convergence of the back-propagation algorithm is very sensitive to the order of presentation of the training set, and to the effective preprocessing of data, such as the resolution of the histograms. Additionally, a very significant amount of processing time is needed, which makes it difficult, for example, to test the influence of the number or the size of hidden layers. Non-determinism may arise in the network, associated with the random setting of connection weights when the network is initialised.

7 Neural Computers

This chapter presents some features of the specifications of future neural computers. The implementation, on real computers, of models described earlier in this volume is very much state of the art. Finally, perspectives offered by new technologies in this domain are discussed and illustrated by the description of a few prototypes.

7.1 Introduction

The application domains of neural networks are largely those linked to perception and artificial intelligence. These are difficult problems whose classical solution are not always completely satisfactory and, above all, are extremely costly in processing time. One method of improving performance is to consider parallel processing. For a particular algorithm, this involves finding a specific formulation so that the algorithm is executable on several processors simultaneously. While this solution may be completely natural, is not always self evident. The parallelisation of a given algorithm is a large amount of work which needs to be carried out from scratch for each new problem.

Networks of artificial neurons allow solutions to certain problems in these application domains to be constructed using a process of learning. These solutions are often of a comparable quality to those obtained by more classical methods. In addition, neural networks are massively parallel: each neuron may be seen as an independent processor with very simple functions.

In conclusion, physical implementations of the models described earlier would enable the ready exploitation of their intrinsic parallelism and would thus make the technology of neural networks immediately available operationally.

7.2 A Model for a General Neural Computer

No true neural computer exists today; nevertheless, we can now give a definition and some significant characteristics of such a device.

A neural computer is fundamentally a set of interconnected processing units, functioning in parallel. Three parameters appear important in classifying the de-

119

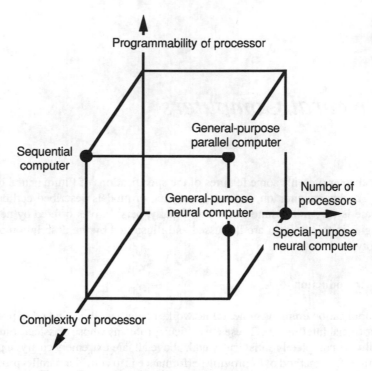

Figure 7.1   Classification of different architectures

vice: the complexity of the elementary unit, which can vary from a simple analogue amplifier to a traditional microprocessor; the number of independent units;
and the level of 'programmability' of the network. This is essentially the potential
for changing the connection graph, the value of the weights of connections and
the mode of communication between the different units.

These parameters allow us to define the full range of architectures which may
be used to implement neural networks: a graphical representation of these alter-
natives is shown in figure 7.1.

Conventional sequential computers with single processors, albeit complex, allow any arbitrary model of a network to be simulated in a fully parameterised
manner. This architecture is especially suitable for experimental purposes. Its
flexibility allows new algorithms to be studied, new applications, different connection graphs for a given application and so on.

Conventional, general purpose parallel computers or vector computers may be
used to simulate a network of neurons.

Specialised neural computers consist of a set of very simple non-programmable
units (analogue gates, for example) connected by a fixed set of connections whose

weights may be variable or fixed. This type of architecture is ideal for well-defined, specific problems in which speed is crucial, for example to implement specialised networks for vision purposes.

General purpose neural computers resemble parallel conventional computers more closely. These use commercial processors but are generally integrated into a hardware architecture specialised for the simulation of networks of neurons.

We shall study an example of each of these architectures.

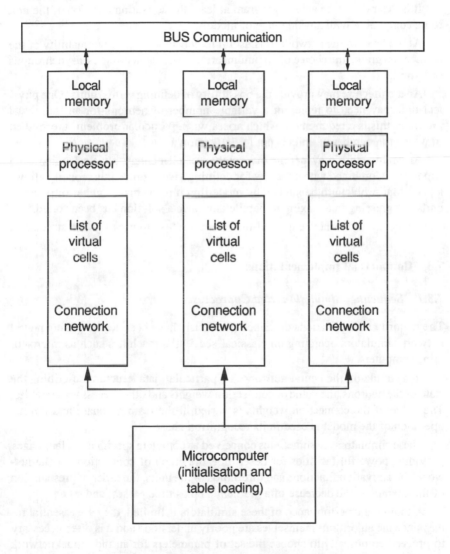

Figure 7.2   Neural computer: block diagram

The following criteria are useful in the search for a satisfactory compromise between performance and flexibility of use.

In the fundamental unit, simplicity is necessary to implement large networks in which thousands or millions of these units are integrated onto a single chip.

To implement networks of an unknown size and an unknown shape with the same units it is necessary that the processor contains the 'hardware' necessary for an autonomous operation such as communications, local memory and calculation hardware.

It is desirable to be able to program at least the activation function of the unit to be compatible with a wide range of models.

At the level of the network, it is useful to consider the programmability of the connection graph, the choice of communication mode, synchronous, asynchronous or hybrid.

An architecture may provide the possibility of defining virtual units. One physical unit may need to represent a variable number of neurons for an individual problem: this is a requirement which arises when particular problems are studied in which the number of units is not initially known.

An architecture may permit the number of elementary physical units to be expanded. Combined with a facility for defining virtual units, this property allows a particular problem to be studied by modelling it on a small number of physical units, progressing to a maximum parallelism once a solution has been found.

Figure 7.2 shows how a general-purpose neural computer might be structured.

7.3   Commercial Implementations

7.3.1   Sequential Simulations and Coprocessors

The majority of applications described previously have been realised using neural network simulators operating on classical sequential machines such as micro- or mini-computers.

In a simulator, the neural network is a particular data structure describing the state of the neurons, the value of connection weights and other necessary variables. The value of the connection weights is varied in the learning phase and normal operation of the model is used in its recognition phase.

These simulators are sometimes conceived as complete specification languages, providing powerful facilities for describing the graph of connections of the network, the activation functions and thresholds of the units, the order of presentation of the examples, the decrease of a gradient step as time passes, and so on.

Although the performance of these simulators is limited, they are essential to-day since the algorithms themselves are poorly understood and it is often necessary to proceed empirically to choose the set of parameters for an individual network to address a particular problem.

Company	Product	Number of units	Number of arcs	Learning speed	Operation speed
Hecht-Nielsen	ANZA	30K	480K	25K	45K
NeuroComputer	ANZA Plus	1M	1.5M	1.5M	6M
Human Devices	Parallon 2	10K	52K	15K	30K
	Parallon 2X	91K	300K	15K	30K
SAIC	SIGMA	1M	1M	2M	11M
Texas Instruments	ODYSSEY	8K	250K	2M	-
TRW	MARK III	8K	400K	300K	-
	MARK IV	236K	5.5M	5M	-

Figure 7.3   Commercial coprocessors and simulators

The suppliers of this software are essentially addressing the problems of network specification, the man-machine interface, the variety of models provided, and other similar factors.

In order to improve the speed performance of these simulators, some of them are supplied with a hardware extension, consisting in general of a specialised processor with fast access to memory.

The principal simulators available today are:

Sigma 1 (SAIC): this is a simulator for the IBM PC, using a card based on a specialised processor to carry out floating point multiplications and additions with 12 megabytes of additional memory. The majority of existing models (about 15) are implemented and a specification language for neural networks, ANSpec, is provided.

ANZA and ANZA Plus, from Hecht Nielsen, are again simulators for the IBM PC, with coprocessor cards based on the Motorola M68020 and M68881 and possessing 4 megabytes of memory. The specification language provided is called AXON.

Mark III and Mark IV, from TRW, consist of a add-on cards for the VME Bus containing 15 M68020 and M68881 processors, supplied with ANSE, a graphical environment for specifying networks.

The performance of a neural network simulator is measured in CUPS, which stands for connection updates per second. This unit measures the number of operations of connections in learning mode with the back-propagation algorithm. The table shown in figure 7.3 (after [Hec]) summarises the performance of different hardware systems.

7.3.2   General Parallel Architectures

Under this heading appear those parallel computers which were designed for general applications. Here we describe two architectures, among the most popular today.

Transputers

Inmos developed the transputer within the framework of an ESPRIT project in 1983. The transputer is designed to be used in parallel configurations, such as that in figure 7.4. In its most complex version this processor has the following characteristics: a power of 10 mips and 2 megaflops, up to 256 kilobytes of local memory, and 4 pairs of uni-directional links which operate at 10 megabits per second. The transputer uses the programming language occam.

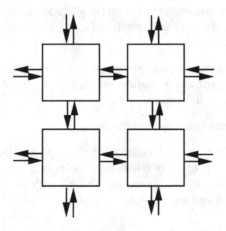

Figure 7.4   Network of 4 transputers

The design of transputers, in particular the provision of only 4 links, prevents their use directly in neural networks as elementary neurons. Their configuration might also present more power than is actually needed. Pseudo-parallelism used in a single processor may allow this difficulty to be overcome, one physical processor playing the role of several virtual processors, each one simulating one neuron.

occam and transputers are becoming standard components in parallel computer research, largely because of their low price, their modularity and their high power.

Today, there are no commercial simulators for neural networks which operate on this architecture; however, the majority of laboratories and industrial workers researching in neural networks use transputer networks.

The Connection Machine

The Connection Machine (described in [Hil]) is a very specialised machine constructed from 65,536 processors in which there are two levels of parallelism. The processors themselves are minimal in that they possess a one-bit register. Sixteen processors are laid out in a square grid. This grid makes up one of 4096 nodes distributed on the corners of a 12 dimension hypercube.

NETTalk was programmed on the connection machine. The result was significant: 200 times faster than on a VAX 780.

7.4 Prototypes and Prospects

7.4.1 Specialised Parallel Architectures

Parallel architectures are today being designed especially for the simulation of neural networks. In general these consist of cards similar to the coprocessors described in section 7.3.1, but they are cascadable in the sense that several cards may be connected to the same host computer.

Here we can mention the development environment for neural networks designed experimentally by IBM, the CONE (computation network environment) system. Cone consists of three elements: a cascadable coprocessor for an IBM PC (NEP, the network emulation processor), a simulation program running on this hardware (IXP, the interactive execution program), and a language for specifying networks (GNL, the generalised network language).

7.4.2 VLSI Neural Computers

Given the simplicity of the artificial neuron in the majority of neural models, it is tempting to think of the direct implementation of a neural network in hardware. The problem which is immediately confronted is that of the number of connections: it is very costly to implement a circuit with high connectivity in VLSI.

Different solutions for this problem have been envisaged.

We may try to decrease the number of neurons. In order to do this, the elementary neuron may need to become more complex. It can be shown that, by defining neurons with several discrete states, it is possible to simulate the operation of a Hopfield network with many fewer units.

Connections whose value varies with time may also be used. Following an idea by Weinfeld and Dreyfus, spatial and temporal connections, implemented using shift registers, are introduced between neurons. The calculation of synaptic potentials is carried out in a number of steps, in parallel for all the neurons. This is shown in figure 7.5.

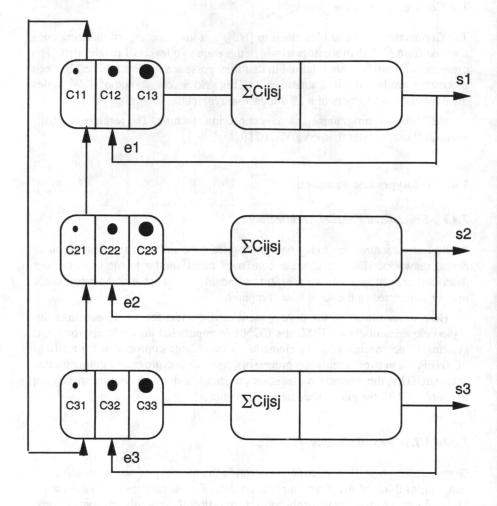

Figure 7.5   Spatial and temporal connection weights

Implementations are still at a very experimental stage. A number of laboratories in the United States have developed prototypes of neural networks in VLSI: AT&T, the Jet Propulsion Laboratory, California Institute of Technology and Bell Communications Research.

Consider the example of one of the chips developed by AT&T. It consists of 54 analogue neurons (amplifiers) in VLSI CMOS technology, with 2,916 programmable connections whose values are held in RAM. The connections occupy 90% of the surface of the chip which is about 6.7 millimetres square, with 75,000 transistors. This circuit implements a model similar to the Hopfield model. With 10 vectors memorised, the convergence time of the circuit from an arbitrary state to a stable state is of the order of 100 nanoseconds, varying between 50 and 600 nanoseconds.

7.4.3 Optical Neural Computers

The problem with implementing neural networks electronically is essentially due to connections: the density of connections in the network and the implementation of dynamic weights. Using a programmable spatial light modulator, Psaltis constructed an optical solution optimised for these facilities.

Optical implementations of neural networks almost always use the Hopfield model for the simplicity of its connection network and for the absence of dynamic connections.

However, optical methods may be applied to other models of networks. Consider figure 7.6, in which N neurons are represented by diodes. The light rays from them are focused by a lens on a light modulator, consisting of a screen whose transparency is non-uniform, having a value which is controlled by the application of an electrical potential at each point. The value of this transparency may be controlled by a microcomputer.

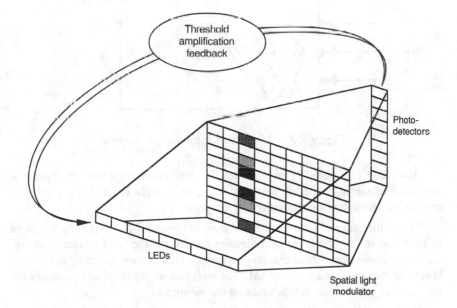

Figure 7.6   Optical neurocomputer

The sum of the luminous intensity weighted by the transparency matrix is cal-culated by making the rays of light converge on photodetectors. This implements the operation of weighted summation.

The operation of thresholding is then carried out electronically and it is then possible to close the loop by returning signals to the LEDs.

7.4.4 Molecular Computers

The principle of molecular processing of information is based on the spatial rela-tionships of enzymes and proteins. In brief, the shape of an enzyme is specialised in order to carry out the 'recognition' of a particular *messenger* in a protein and to implement its transformation.

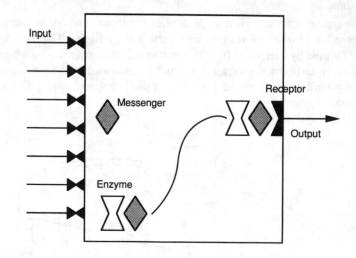

Figure 7.7   Molecular computer: principles

According to Conrad [Con], the key for molecular computers is the trans-formation of signals (whether electrical impulses or light signals) into particular molecules which may be recognised by enzymes.

The architecture of such a system, shown in figure 7.7 (from [Con]), might be in three layers. A first layer of molecules transforms the light or electrical sig-nals into messengers. These messengers are selectively recognised by the second layer, the enzymes, and transformed. The enzymes of the third layer identify the transformed messengers and produce an output signal.

This technology is still at the level of fundamental research: some models exist but there are no real implementations. The first elementary molecular components might appear within perhaps 10 years.

7.5 Summary

Models of networks of neurons are still relatively poorly understood both theoretically and practically. Extensive use of these models on a wide variety of real applications is necessary.

Neural network simulators, functioning on sequential computers, quickly become unsuitable for the implementation of significant applications given the speed of calculation needed by these models. For this reason exploitation of the intrinsic parallelism in neural networks is needed.

An imminent development is the availability of a range of general-purpose parallel architectures, such as those based upon transputers, independent of the needs of neural networks. These architectures will probably enable the first generation of neural computers to be built.

In the longer term, more specialised architectures will appear. These architectures are experimental today: VLSI neural computers, optical or holographic devices, even molecular computers.

In this manner, neural networks, supported by ever improved hardware, both more suitable and more powerful, will be better studied and better understood and can become a true new technology.

Appendix A *Back-propagation Rule*

We consider a network with N input neurons, M output neurons and an arbitrary number of hidden layers. We assume that neuron outputs are connected only to later neurons, in the sense from input to output, but not necessarily those in the immediately following layer. The architecture is shown in figure A.1.

The notation used is shown in figure A.2, and is as follows:

X $(X_1, X_2, X_3, \ldots, X_n)$ input vector
Y $(Y_1, Y_2, Y_3, \ldots, Y_m)$ desired output vector
S $(S_1, S_2, S_3, \ldots, S_m)$ actual obtained output vector
f the sigmoid activation function of a neuron
f' the derivative of the activation function
O_j the output of neuron j
I_j the input of neuron i
$e(k)$ the step size at iteration k

The total error on the outputs when one training example is presented is calculated:

$$E^k(W) = (S^k - Y^k)^2 = \sum_{i=1,m} (S_i^k - Y_i^k)^2$$

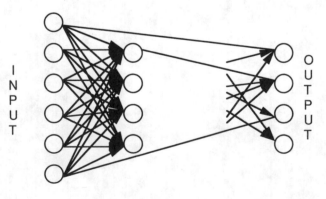

Figure A.1   Architecture of network

130

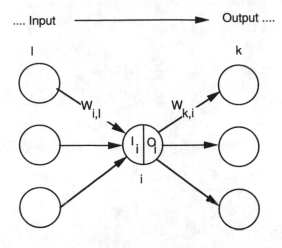

.... Input   ⟶   Output ....

Figure A.2   Notation

The total error over the complete training set is then calculated:

$$E(W) = \sum_k E^k(W)$$

The back-propagation algorithm consists of carrying out a gradient descent minimisation process on E. In general, an approximation may be used, in which each connection weight is modified following each presentation of example k, using changes given by:

$$W_{ij}(k) = W_{ij}(k-1) - e(k)\frac{\delta E^k}{\delta W_{ij}}$$

This necessitates calculating the sensitivity of E^k to each weight W_{ij}:

$$\frac{\delta E^k}{\delta W_{ij}} = \frac{\delta E^k}{\delta I_i}\frac{\delta I_i}{\delta W_{ij}}$$

Alternatively,

$$\frac{\delta I_i}{\delta W_{ij}} = \frac{\delta(\sum_p W_{ip}O_p)}{\delta W_{ij}} = O_j$$

In the latter formulation, p ranges over the neurons in the layer preceding neuron i, and the outputs O_p of these neurons do not depend on the weights W_{ij}.

A result for the error sensitivity is obtained:

$$\frac{\delta E^k}{\delta W_{ij}} = \frac{\delta E^k}{\delta I_i}O_j$$

Substituting d_i for $\dfrac{\delta E^k}{\delta I_i}$, we obtain:

$$\frac{\delta E^k}{\delta W_{ij}} = d_i O_j$$

giving:

$$W_{ij}(k) = W_{ij}(k-1) - e(k)d_i O_j$$

For a neuron i in the output layer, since only S_i^k depends on I_i we have:

$$d_i = \frac{\delta \left[\sum_j (S_j^k - Y_j^k)^2 \right]}{\delta I_i} = 2(S_i^k - Y_i^k)\frac{\delta S_i^k}{\delta I_i}$$

Furthermore, since $S_i^k = f(I_i)$:

$$d_i = 2(S_i^k - Y_i^k)f'(I_i)$$

For the neurons in hidden layers:

$$d_i = \sum_h \frac{\delta E^k}{\delta I_h}\frac{\delta I_h}{\delta I_i} = \sum_h d_h \frac{\delta I_h}{\delta I_i}$$

In this equation, h ranges over the neurons to which neuron i sends signals. In reality, the inputs I_h to other neurons are independent of I_i. This means that:

$$d_i = \sum_h d_h \frac{\delta I_h}{\delta O_i}\frac{\delta O_i}{\delta I_i}$$

Using an index p over neurons providing input to h, these neurons are contained in the same layer as i and thus their outputs O_p are independent of O_i for $p \neq i$, giving:

$$\frac{\delta I_h}{\delta O_i} = \frac{\delta(\sum_p W_{hp}O_p)}{\delta O_i} = W_{hi}$$

Finally, since $O_i = f(I_i)$, we obtain:

$$d_i = \sum_h d_h W_{hi} f'(I_i)$$

This gives the complete rule for modifying weights, when an example from the training set is presented for the k'th time:

$$W_{ij}(k) = W_{ij}(k-1) - e(k)d_i O_j$$

$$d_i = 2(S_i - Y_i)f'(I_i) \quad \text{(output layer)}$$
$$d_i = \sum_h d_h W_{hi} f'(I_i) \quad \text{(hidden layers)}$$

Appendix B *The Kohonen Model - Formal Description*

B.1 Algorithm for a 2-dimensional Autonomous System

o Find the weight vector closest to the input vector:

$$| E - M_c | = \min_j(| E - M_j |)$$

o Modify the weights:

$$M_i(t) = \begin{cases} M_i(t-1) + a(t)[E(t) - M_i(t-1)] & \text{for neurons } i \text{ in } V_c \\ M_i(t-1) & \text{for neurons } i \text{ outside } V_c \end{cases}$$

B.2 Algorithm for Travelling Salesman Problem

o Find the weight vector closest to the input vector:

$$| E - M_c | = \min_j(| E - M_j |)$$

o Modify the weights.
For each neuron i, we have the following formula:

$$M_i(t) = M_i(t-1) + f(a, d)[E(t) - M_i(t-1)]$$

Here, a is a *gain* parameter, and d is the distance between neuron i and neuron c. (d is an integer lying between 0 and $n - 1$.)

$$f(a, d) = \frac{1}{\sqrt{2}} \exp(-d^2/a)$$

The gain decreases after each cycle of presentation of each town, using $a \leftarrow (1 - q)a$. Different values for q, varying between 0.02 and 0.2, have been investigated in [Ang]. The gain decreases from a high value, allowing large modifications to the weights, to a very small value as the network reaches a stable state.

B.3   The Pseudo-inverse: the Penrose Algorithm

Different investigations have attempted to find algorithms to calculate the inverse matrix required by the Moore-Penrose algorithm. Kalaba and Rasakhoo, in 'Algorithms for General Inverses,' give an algorithm which is highly attractive for its simplicity.

Given Z is a matrix of m rows and n columns of order r, the Moore-Penrose matrix Z^+ obeys the following relations:

$$Z^+.Z.Z^+ = Z^+$$
$$Z.Z^+.Z = Z$$
$$(Z^+.Z)^T = Z^+.Z$$
$$(Z.Z^+)^T = Z.Z^+$$

A collection of lemmas are given below, leading to a theorem which gives the basis of a calculation algorithm.

Lemma B.1 Z may be written in the form:

$$Z = d1.w1.v1^T + d2.w2.v2^T + \cdots + dr.wr.vr^T$$

where

$$0 \le dr \le \ldots \le d2 \le d1$$

$\{w1, w2, \ldots, wr\}$ is a system orthogonal to R^m, and $\{v1, v2, \ldots, vr\}$ is a system orthogonal to R^n

Lemma B.2 Z^+ is given by:

$$Z^+ = 1/d1.v1.w1^T + \cdots + 1/dr.vr.wr^T$$

Lemma B.3 Z^+ may also be written:

$$Z^+ = \lim_{\beta \to 0} [(Z^+.Z + \beta.Id)^{-1}.Z^T]$$

Lemma B.4 With:

$$A = \mathrm{adj}(Z^T.Z + \beta.Id) = A_1.\beta^{n-1} + \cdots + A_{n-1}.\beta + A_n$$

$$delta = \det(Z^T.Z + \beta.Id) = delta_0.\beta^n + \cdots + delta_{n-1}.\beta + delta_n$$

where $A_1, A_2, \ldots, A_n$ are $n \times n$ matrices independent of β and $delta_0, delta_1, \ldots, delta_n$ are scalars.

This gives:

$$Z^+ = (A_l/delta_l).Z^T$$

where l is the largest index such that $delta_i \ne 0$.

Theorem B.1 The items $A_1, A_2, \ldots, A_n$ and $delta_0, delta_1, \ldots, delta_n$ are calculated using the following recurrence relations:

$$A_{k+1} = delta_k Id + Z^T.Z.A_k$$

$$delta_{k+1} = \frac{1}{(k+1)} trace(Z^T.Z.A_{k+1})$$

with $k = 1, 2, \ldots, n-1$ and initial conditions $A_1 = Id$ and $delta_0 = trace(Z^T.Z)$.

B.4 Learning Algorithm for Pattern Recognition

The network is initialised as follows:

- o each class is assigned to a group of neurons proportional in number to the *a priori* probability of this class appearing in the input set
- o the weight vectors are initialised using the first examples from the training set; each weight vector takes the value of one input vector which lies in the class of inputs represented by this group of neurons
- o having assigned each neuron to a class of inputs, the weights are subsequently modified as successive further examples from the training set are presented
- o every time a new example E is presented, it is compared against all the weight vectors, and one vector W_c, the closest to E is chosen.

If E_t and neuron c belong to the same class, the weights are modified by:

$$W_c(t+1) = W_c(t) + k(t)[E(t) - W_c(t)]$$

If E_t and neuron c belong to different classes, the weights are modified by:

$$W_c(t+1) = W_c(t) - k(t)[E(t) - W_c(t)]$$

For all $i \neq c$, the weights remain unchanged:

$$W_i(t+1) = W_i(t)$$

The term $k(t)$ is a positive parameter which decreases with increasing t. For example, to ensure convergence in a finite time, one might use $k(t) = a - bt \geq 0$.

References

[Ack] D. H. Ackley, G. E. Hinton and T. J. Sejnowski, "A Learning Algorithm for Boltzmann Machines," *Cognitive Science*, Vol 9, pp 147-169, 1985.

[Ami] Daniel J. Amit, Harroch Gutfreund and H. Sompolinsky, "Spin-glass Models of Neural Networks", *Physical Review A*, Volume 32, number 2.

[Ang] Bernard Angéniol, Gaël de La Croix Vaubois and Jean-Yves Le Texier, "Self-organising Feature Maps and the Travelling Salesman Problem," *Actes de Neuro-Nîmes*, November, 1988.

[Bai] D. L. Bailey, D. M. Thomson and J. L. Feinstein, "Options Tradings using Neural Networks," *NeuroNîmes*, November, 1988.

[Bar] A. G. Barto, R. S. Sutton and C. W. Anderson, "Neuronlike Adaptive Elements that can Solve Difficult Learning Control Problems," *IEEE Transactions on Systems, Man, and Cybernetics*, Vol SMC-13, No. 5, 1983.

[Bur] Yves Burnod, *An Adaptive Neural Network: The Cerebral Cortex*, Masson.

[Chan] Jean-Pierre Changeux, *L'homme Neuronal*, Pluriel.

[Chap] Georges Chapoutier, Michel Kreutzer and Christian Menini, *Le Système Nerveux et le Comportement*, Etudes Vivantes, collection Academic Press.

[Coc] Yves Cochet and Gérard Paget, "Neural Networks for Images Databases," *International Neural Networks Society First Annual Meeting*, Boston MA, September, 1988.

[Col] E. Collins, S. Ghosh and C. Scofield, "An Application of a Multiple Neural Network Learning System to Emulation of Mortgage Underwriting," Nestor Inc., 1 Richmond Square, Providence R.I. 02906.

[Con] M. Conrad, "The Lure of Molecular Computing," *IEEE Spectrum*, Vol 23, No. 10, pp 55-60, 1986.

[Coo] L. Cooper, F. Liberman and E. Oja, "A Theory for the Acquisition and Loss of Neuron Specificity in Visual Cortex", *Biol. Cybernetics*, Number 33, pages 9-28 (1979).

[Cun]   Y. Le Cun, *Modèles Connexionnistes de l'Apprentissage,* Doctorate thesis, University of Paris 6.

[Cun2]   Y. Le Cun, "Une Procédure d'Aprentissage pour Réseau à Seuil Asymétrique," *Proceedings of Cognitiva 85,* pp 599-604, Paris.

[Def]   G. Deffuant, *Neural Units Recruitment Algorithms for Generation of Decision Trees,* 1990.

[Del]   J. Delacour and A. Danchin, *Neurobiologie de l'Apprentissage,* Masson.

[Fog]   F. Fogelman Soulié, *Le Connexionnisme,* notes for MARI 87 course, Cognitiva 87.

[Fuk1]   Kunihiko Fukushima, Sei Miyake and Takayuki Ito, "Neorecognitron: a Neural Network Model for a Mechanism of Visual Pattern Recognition," *IEEE Transactions on Systems, Man and Cybernetics,* Vol. SMC-13, pp 826-834.

[Fuk2]   Kunihiko Fukushima, "Neorecognitron: A Self-organizing Neural Network Model for a Mechanism of Pattern Recognition Unaffected by Shift in Position," *Biological Cybernetics,* Vol. 36, pp 193-202.

[Goy]   Pierre Goyeneix, *Actes de Neuro-Nîmes,* November 1988.

[Heb]   D. O. Hebb, *The Organisation of Behaviour,* Wiley, New York, 1949.

[Hec]   R. Hecht-Nielsen, "Neurocomputing: Picking the Human Brain," *IEEE Spectrum,* Vol 25, no. 3, pp 36-41, 1988.

[Hil]   W. D. Hillis, *The Connection Machine,* MIT Press, 1985.

[Hin]   G. E. Hinton, "Implementing Semantic Networks in Parallel Hardware," in G. E. Hinton and J. A. Anderson (eds.), *Parallel models of associative memory,* pp 161-188, Erlbaum, Hillsdale, NJ, 1981.

[Ho1]   J. J. Hopfield, "Neural Networks and Physical Systems with Emergent Collective Computational Abilities," *Proceedings of the National Academy of Sciences, USA,* Vol. 79, pp 2554-2558, 1982.

[Ho2]   J. J. Hopfield, "Neurons With Graded Response Have Collective Computational Properties Like Those of Two-state Neurons," *Proceedings of the National Academy of Sciences, USA,* Vol. 81, pp 3088-3092, 1984

[Ho3]   J. J. Hopfield, D. I. Feinstein and R. G. Palmer, "Unlearning Has a Stabilizing Effect in Collective Memories," *Nature,* Vol. 304, pp 158-159, 1983.

[Ho4]   J. J. Hopfield and D. W. Tank "Neural Computation of Decisions in Optimisation Problems," *Biological Cybernetics,* Vol. 52, pp 141-152, 1985.

[Kir]   S. Kirkpatrick, C. D. Gelatt and M. P. Vecchi, "Optimisation by Simulated Annealing," *Science,* Vol 220, pp 671-680, 1983.

[Koh]   T. Kohonen, *Self-organization and Associative Memory,* Springer-Verlag, Berlin, 1984.

[Koh2]   T. Kohonen, "An Introduction to Neural Computing," *Neural Networks*, Vol. 1, no. 1, 1988.

[McCl]   J. L. McClelland and D. E. Rumelhart, *Parallel Distributed Processing*, *Vol. 2*, MIT Press.

[McCu]   W. S. McCulloch and W. Pitts, "A Logical Calculus of the Ideas Immanent in Nervous Activity," *Bulletin of Mathematical Biophysics*, Vol 5, pp 115-133, 1943.

[Mes]   J. B. Messenger, "Nerves, Brains and Behaviour", in *Studies in biology no. 114.*

[Met]   N. Metropolis, A. W. Rosenbluth, M. N. Rosenbluth, A. H. Teller and E. Teller, "Equation of State Calculations for Fast Computing Machines," *Journal of Chemical Physics*, Vol 6, p 1087, 1953.

[Mez]   M Mézard and S. Nadal, "Learning in Feedforward Neural Networks: the Tiling Algorithm," *J. Phys. A: Math. Gen.*, 1990.

[Min]   M. Minsky and S. Papert, *Perceptrons: an Introduction to Computational Geometry*, MIT Press, 1969.

[Nad]   J. P. Nadal, "Study of a Growth Algorithm for a Feedforward Network," *International Journal of Neural Systems*, Vol. 1, no. 1.

[Nad2]   J. P. Nadal, G. Toulouse, J. P. Changeux and S. Dehaene, "Networks of Formal Neurons and Memory Palimpsests," *Europhysics Letters*, 1(10), pp 353-542, 1986.

[Per]   L. Personnaz, I. Guyon and G. Dreyfus, "Collective Computational Properties of Neural Networks: New Learning Mechanisms," *Physical Review A*, Vol. 34, No. 3, 1986.

[Per1]   P. Peretto, "Collective properties of Neural Networks: a Statistical Physics Approach", *Biol. Cybernetics*, Number 50, pp 51-62, 1984.

[Per2]   Pierre Peretto and Jean-Jacques Niez, "Stochastic Dynamics of Neural Networks", *IEEE Transactions on Systems, Man, and Cybernetics, vol. SMC-16, no. 1.*

[Pop]   G. Pöppel and U. Krey, "Dynamical Learning Process for Recognition of Correlated Patterns in Symmetric Spin Glass Models," *Europhysics Letters*, 4(9), pp 979-985, 1987.

[Ros1]   F. Rosenblatt, "The Perceptron: a Probabilistic Model for Information Storage and Organisation in the Brain," *Psychological Review*, Vol 65, pp 386-408.

[Ros2]   F. Rosenblatt, *Principles of Neurodynamics*, Spartan, New York, 1962.

[Ru1]   D. E. Rumelhart, G. E. Hinton and R. J. Williams, "Learning Internal Representations by Error Propagation," in D. E. Rumelhart and J. L. McClelland (Eds.), *Parallel Distributed Processing: Explorations in the Microstructures of Cognition, Vol. 1: Foundations*. MIT Press, 1986.

[Ru2]   D. E. Rumelhart, G. E. Hinton and R. J. Williams, "Learning Representations by Back-propagating Errors," *Nature*, Vol. 323, pp 533-536, 1986.

[Ru3]   D. E. Rumelhart and J. L. McClelland, "On Learning Past Tenses of English Verbs," *Parallel Distributed Processing: Explorations in the Microstructures of Cognition, Vol. 2.* MIT Press, 1986.

[Sej]   T. J. Sejnowski and C. R. Rosenberg, *NETTalk: a Parallel Network That Learns to Read Aloud,* Johns Hopkins University Technical Report JHU/EECS-86/01, 32pp.

[Vin]   Jean-Didier Vincent, *Biologie des Passions,* Points.

[Wic]   W. A. Wickelgren, "Context, Sensitive Coding, Associative Memory, and Serial Order in (Speech) Behaviour," *Psychological Review,* Vol 76, pp 1-15, 1969.

[Wid]   B. Widrow and M. E. Hoff, "Adaptive Switching Circuits," *1960 IRE WESCON Conv Record, Part 4,* pp 96-104.

Index